HARVEST

CHUCK SMITH
& TAL BROOKE

W9-BMP-317

THE WORD
FOR TODAY

The Word For Today • PO Box 8000, Costa Mesa, CA 92628
800-272-WORD (9673)
Web site: www.twft.com • E-mail: info@twft.com

HARVEST
by Chuck Smith and Tal Brooke

Copyright © 1987, 2005, 2010 by The Word For Today
P.O. Box 8000, Costa Mesa, CA 92628

Eighth printing

Web Site: www.twft.com
E-mail: info@twft.com

ISBN 13: 978-0–936728–42–1

Edited by Scott Richards

Printed in the United States of America

Contents

FOREWORD

One of the constant frustrations that we as Christians face is that of seeking to know the unknowable. We would like to figure out God's ways. Yet God Himself has said, "My ways are not your ways; My ways are beyond your finding out."

When God desired to bring the nation Israel to the apex of its power, He chose an unlikely person to lead them to this place of glory. From the house of Jesse, in the city of Bethlehem, He anointed the youngest son, a boy named David, whose only qualifications were that he was a shepherd who loved God and reflected on His greatness as it was revealed in nature.

When God wanted to raise up a mighty army for David, He gathered those who were distressed, in debt, and discontented. These unlikely soldiers became David's mighty men and through them, God achieved remarkable victories.

When Jesus wanted to turn the world upside-down by bringing the message of God's love to all mankind, He chose unlikely candidates. Of the twelve, most were fishermen and one was a hated publican. These are certainly not the choices the average person would have made for the task. When God wanted to make an impact on our society, He again chose the foolish things (as far as the world is concerned) to confound the wise; He chose the weak things to confound the mighty.

For instance, in raising up pastors to shepherd Calvary Chapel churches with thousands of members, God did not necessarily look for Phi Beta Kappas from Yale or Harvard. He did not look for magna cum laude graduates with impressive resumés. Instead, God chose people like a Mexican street fighter who had dropped out of high school, a hippie who had gone insane on drugs, a drug dealer who was into sorcery, and a motorcycle gang member to build His churches in the Calvary Chapel movement. God has used many such unlikely leaders to turn worn traditions up~ide-down.

In these pages, you are going to read the incred
almost unbelievable accounts of men with varied, v
Satanic backgrounds, with one thing in commo

touched by the grace of God and now are being used to touch thousands of other lives. As you read, you will no doubt wonder how these men, who for the most part had no formal education for the ministry, were able to go out and build churches ranging in size from several thousand to ten thousand members.

What are the common factors? What are the things they learned that enabled them to experience such phenomenal success in their ministries? The stories you will read are only a sampling of the scores of others that we have watched come into our church over the years, but are uniquely representative of the transforming work of the Spirit of God.

We are convinced that the concepts that the Lord has taught us in forty years of ministry are transferable to others. If followed, these principles can help build strong churches all over the country.

In the book of Acts, we read that at the birth of the Church 3,000 souls came to Christ the very first day. Then the Lord continued to add daily such as should be saved. We are convinced that when the Church becomes what God intended it to be, God will do through the Church what He has always desired to do. Through the power of His grace He will bring in a harvest of souls that can only humble our loftiest plans. Indeed, His ways are not always our ways. He desires to bless us if we will only but hear His voice.

Chuck Smith
Calvary Chapel of Costa Mesa

PREFACE

I blotted my forehead and opened recent copies of *Look*, *Time*, and *Newsweek* magazines. Full-page photographs held me spellbound.

Sweat dripped down my arms as I stood holding the magazines in a hot crowded South Indian bazaar. I was at a roadside stand near the Bangalore bus station in Mysore State. I was returning to the headquarters of Sai Baba, the most influential guru in India. At the time, I was a member of his inner circle.

A human form almost jumped out of one picture: a glistening body was plunging up from the Pacific Ocean, his arms outstretched toward the blue heavens above. It was a microsecond frozen in time. Particles of ocean spray hung crystallized in space. Water, frozen like glass, cascaded down his torso. A million droplets beaded his skin like jewels. His face seemed to hold an ocean of joyous ecstasy. Blissful relief had turned his countenance into a smiling cathedral of hope.

Here was a vintage California hippie, tanned with long golden hair that clung to a lean, muscular chest. The road map of this fellow's past could still be seen in his veins and face. He had experienced everything from shooting drugs in Haight Ashbury to eating sun-ripened fruit and thumbing along Route 1 between San Francisco and L.A. Yet the face coming out of the ocean indicated that the journey had come to a joyous and unexpected end. No more striving. No more hell. Infinite peace rested on this fortunate soul.

The young man in the picture had just been baptized in a cove at Corona Del Mar Beach. He had made an incredible journey from Golden Gate to eternity. He was one of nine hundred people baptized that day by Calvary Chapel. The Jesus Movement was going full-gear on the California coast.

The main figure performing the baptisms in the other pictures was Chuck Smith, the man behind the Calvary Chapel phenomenon that was sweeping the West Coast and other parts of America. For months, this fellowship had been baptizing an average of nine hundred people a month. It was a phenomenon that was bewildering the secular pundits, from Marcuse to Leary.

The pictures indicated that the crowd standing in the Pacific and along the rock bluff had abandoned the dreams of the counterculture to become Christians, casting their lives and burdens on Jesus Christ. They had abandoned the whole parcel of wild pleasures and freedoms—drugs, communal living, rejection of social norms, free sex, and all of the Eastern spiritualities that tagged along with this radical life experiment—in order to adopt Christianity, of all things. From my point of view in India, the pictures suggested a serious setback. The old world biblical view, with its black and white paradigms, was getting a new foothold. Why? Sooner than I dared think I would know the answer to that question.

For two years, I had been in India following the "consciousness expansion" regimen of a self-proclaimed God-man, who told me that I was destined for enlightenment. I was riding the crest of a mystical wave that would help bring the New Age movement to America in the coming ten years. It was a real-life drama that had all the intrigue of an adventure movie. But the magazine picture before me was an affront to all that I believed. It signaled opposition to the gathering momentum of our "new consciousness."

As I focused on the picture, I reflected on the enormous difficulty of my own spiritual path toward "godhood." At that time I had been feeling the road-weariness and discouragement that can come from the Eastern spiritual path. To make matters worse some spiritual "tests" impeded my path—in the form of two Christian missionaries. Their love was disquieting. They literally radiated a wholesome goodness. To my surprise even in the most adverse of circumstances, they rejoiced. They had a hidden spring of love and hope that never seemed to yield to personal difficulty. But as for me, even in my "advanced state of consciousness", I often found myself cursing all the things that sullied my trail to eternal perfection.

The *Look* magazine February 1971 cover story that had caught my eye, captured a surprising social phenomenon. The '60s era was dividing up into a number of diverse social highways as it was coming to a close. The counterculture was being portrayed in the picture—but there was a surprise fork in the road. California's radical hippie culture, embodied by the rejoicing nomad in the picture, was suddenly caught in a strange juxtaposition. A photograph of a flower child dripping in the Pacific surf was no surprise, but the reason for his being there was!

Within a year of that quiet moment at the Indian roadside stand, I (like the fellow pictured in the magazine) would be submerged in a lake near Charlottesville, Virginia, and come out with the same smile of relief and joy. For the first time in my life I would know real hope.

Little did I know at the time that, not only would I abandon my guru, but I would become a Christian. And in time I would even end up working with the same central figure in the photographs, Chuck Smith. The article was like God's quiet signal to my soul saying, "You think you are on the path to truth but you have been seduced into believing the most subtle lie in the world. Do you see that figure standing in the waves? That is My servant Chuck Smith. Someday, by My timetable, you will link up with him in the fellowship of ministry."

But that was in the future. At the time I only knew that, along with most of my generation, I had rejected the Christian alternative.

How did it happen? How did we get off the track in the first place? In some ways I was a model case.

A GENERATION IN CHAOS

I grew up in an atheistic home, however that spiritual vacuum would soon be filled by the occult. While my father was a diplomat in London—I was ten years old—he took me up on a dare one evening and brought home a Ouija board with which to experiment. As a convinced materialist he was convinced that all I was doing was engaging in a harmless superstition.

By the time I was an undergraduate at the University of Virginia, I was deeply into mysticism. The door blew open for me when I took a massive dose of Sandoz LSD in the Virginia countryside. It was one of those warm spring evenings when the meadows seemed like a vast armchair. After communicating with what I thought were higher celestial powers, I was certain that I had been given a glimpse of eternity. No one could keep me away from the Upanishads and other Indian holy books. I had a gut-directed sense that one day I would go to India in search of an enlightened master.

But the mystical experience wasn't my sole motivation for turning to Eastern spirituality. One of the key reasons for rejecting Christianity was what I saw in the churches I tried attending. The love that is so enthrallingly reported in the New Testament Church wasn't very evident in those modern churches. In fact its absence was louder than thunder. A small-minded judgmentalism accompanied a chilly aloofness. I felt that even the more conservative churches were not willing to share what they had with anyone who did not meet their particular standards.

To an outsider, there is nothing more sordid than when the grace and beauty of God have departed from a church. What remains is the outward display of religion without the inner heart and soul. Thus, Christianity became irrelevant in my eyes.

But this rejection of the truth was not simply the fault of closed-minded churches. My generation fell into its own trap. The wild permissiveness of the counterculture thought itself more honest in its own eyes than the "judgmental hypocrisy" it saw in the church. We wrote off the church prematurely. So, like my counterparts, I looked upon the overtures of Christianity with acute suspicion. For instance, I submitted the two missionaries I met in India to ruthless scrutiny. Yet what shone out of these two faithful souls was the unhindered grace of God. I reached the end of my road when I encountered the genuine article of God's grace. The caricature of the Church could no longer be an excuse for me. Indeed, during some of my drier years as a professing Christian, I too could be accused of the very things I hated most in the Church. I too was often intolerant, judgmental, and unloving.

To say the least, it takes a powerful ministry to reach a group as alienated and hostile to Christianity as the youth of the '60s and '70s. Amazingly, when these people encountered the ministry of Calvary Chapel, what they saw was enough to disarm them and turn them around.

When I finally strolled into the airy sanctuary of Calvary Chapel of Costa Mesa ten years after my conversion, what I felt was like a refreshing breeze. An abundant flow of love was present everywhere. There was not even a fleeting hint of judgmentalism. Rather, I felt a terrific sense of belonging. I noticed something else about the man in the pulpit. I had long wondered about God's promise that out of His people would flow rivers of living water. Without any question, I saw this happen as Chuck Smith spoke. I saw this as God's seal on the work. Chuck Smith was abundantly blessed as he pointed to God and never to himself.

When I met Chuck Smith after the service, it was like meeting an old friend. Many people thronged in line to meet him (attendance of the three Sunday morning services numbered in the thousands each). When my turn came to meet him, I am not sure I have ever encountered anyone more gracious, open, and loving. I could see why God used this humble soul to reach an entire generation. I also knew that his ministry was not just limited to reaching just one particular age group.

Calvary Chapel started from a humble base. But its strength was its willingness to reach out in a relevant way to a dying generation. The result is perhaps the greatest harvest of souls by a single church in American history. There are some exciting lessons in this for all of us. These are the lessons this book hopes to pursue.

Tal Brooke

CHAPTER
1

In The Beginning

As I describe to you the explosion of church growth that happened in the Calvary Chapel movement, I speak as a spectator. If there is any credit to be given, it belongs to God alone. If you understand this perspective, then when I describe to you my difficult years, my desert years, you will know why I stand in awe at what God has done. And you will celebrate with me the awesome symmetry of God's design. It leaves us all stunned and amazed.

Those pictures in *Look, Life, Time,* and *Newsweek* magazines of our massive Calvary Chapel baptisms in the Pacific Ocean resemble a human harvest field. Literally thousands of people can be seen crowding the shores waiting to be baptized. Images like these illustrate that this is a colossal phenomenon as far as churches go. Professors such as Peter Wagner at Fuller Seminary and Ron Enroth at Westmont College state in their books that there may be nothing like it in American history.

It has been estimated that in a two-year period in the mid-'70s, Calvary Chapel of Costa Mesa had performed well over eight thousand baptisms. During that same period, we were instrumental in 20,000 conversions to the Christian faith. Our decadal growth rate had been calculated by church growth experts to be near the ten thousand percent level.

Perhaps more staggering still is that when we first came to Calvary Chapel church in Costa Mesa in 1965, we had twenty-five people our first Sunday morning.

Now put this in perspective. Not only has that church of twenty-five members established more than a thousand affiliate Calvary Chapels across the world, but that one fellowship in Costa Mesa has grown until the number of people who consider it their home church is more than thirty-five thousand! It is currently listed as number three, according to Sunday attendance, among the ten largest churches in the United States; and is number one of the ten largest Protestant churches in California.

I have heard critics try to dismiss the impact of Calvary Chapel by calling it "production line religion". They have accused us of catering to what people want to hear by diluting the message of Christ to appeal to the masses. Some critics, apparently, have decided what God can and cannot do—and He cannot do "the impossible."

Other critics, who belong to churches that have not grown in years (which was exactly my situation for well over a decade) often adopt a stance of spiritual elitism. To them, smallness proves spirituality, faithfulness, or an unwillingness to compromise. Perhaps they feel that "quantity" diminishes the "quality" of spirituality.

Christ talked about the man who buried his talents and wound up with nothing, because even what he had was taken away. But He also spoke positively about the servant who magnified his talents a thousandfold. So to say that Christ purposefully limits the size and impact of a ministry is unfounded. The explosive force of a ministry can equally be taken as a sign that God is genuinely at work. Who can forget the day of Pentecost when three thousand turned to Christ on the streets of Jerusalem? "And the Lord added to their number daily those who were being saved" (Acts 2:47).

Just as the Jews soon discovered that they were not to keep the Good News among themselves, but were to include the "despised" Gentiles, so there was an interesting shifting of gears at Calvary Chapel. Our fellowship began with twenty-five members who represented mainline, traditional America. Yet God called us to share with the youth from the counterculture. This outreach took a miracle of love and acceptance. But as each group accepted the other, both sides grew in number. There was a vital sense of God stepping into the picture and as lives changed before our eyes. The sense of being in the middle of a miracle kept feeding itself like a bonfire. When some hopeless heroin addict throws away the needle and goes to the beach to convert three people to Christ in an afternoon, it's a pretty strong boost to the faith of everyone involved!

Another remarkable pattern kept repeating itself. As soon as we moved into a new building, our fellowship would already be too big for the facilities. We seemed to grow like a Chinese checker jumping across the board. In two years we moved from our original building (one of the first church buildings in Costa Mesa) to a rented Lutheran church overlooking the Pacific. Soon thereafter we decided to do something unprecedented at the time and move the church to a school that we had bought. The building did not match up to code so we tore it down and built another, hippies and straights working and smiling side by side. It was such a sight that cars on the highway would slow down and gawk at us.

I had always felt that the ideal church size was about 275 and so we built accordingly. But by the time the sanctuary of 330 seats was completed in 1969, we were already forced to go to two services, and eventually had to use the outside courtyard for 500 more seats. This was all fine in good weather.

But by 1971 the large crowds and the winter rains forced us to move again. We bought a ten-acre tract of land on the Costa Mesa/Santa Ana border. Orange County was quickly changing and the once-famous orange orchards were making way for the exploding population of Los Angeles. Soon after buying the land, we again did the unprecedented and erected a giant circus tent that could seat 1,600 at a stretch. This was soon enlarged to hold 2,000 seats. Meanwhile we began building an enormous sanctuary adjacent to this site.

This was all amazing to me and a bit frightening. I would sit at the signal across the street looking at the bare lot that we had obligated ourselves to purchase, and start to panic. It would take a tremendous amount of money to develop the property. Was I being foolish to obligate these people to that kind of a project? Why not be satisfied where you are? The bills are all paid. You've got money in the bank. This is going to take such a great outlay. But then, as I sat there, the Lord spoke to my heart: *Whose church is it?* I replied out loud, "It's Your church, Lord." *Then why are you worried about bankruptcy?*

What an incredible relief. A sense of frantic worry just rolled off my shoulders. The finances were not my responsibility. They were His. This was an extremely important lesson for me to learn. It is not my church. It's His church. And God was the one who had created the problem! He was the one who brought so many people in that we couldn't house them.

God continued to bring people in. By the time Calvary Chapel fellowship had celebrated opening day in 1973 moving into the vast new sanctuary of 2,200 seats, the building was already too small to contain the numbers turning out. We held three Sunday morning services and had more than 4,000 people at each one. Many had to sit on the carpeted floor. A large portion of floor space was left without pews so as to provide that option.

I have always felt it important to maintain a sense of intimate fellowship. For this reason, the building was designed with pillars and beams that break up the sanctuary into segments of two hundred to five hundred seats so that each person has the feeling of being in a congregation rather than in a large crowded auditorium. Even the seating available on the carpeted floor near the front gives a sense of relaxation not unlike sitting in a meadow. The front platform is simple and unornamented. The seats form a semi-circle, communicating that no one is more important than anyone else. It gives an air of fresh openness. Though vast, it avoids pretension.

I keep abreast of all of the details of daily work at Calvary Chapel. I have also instructed my pastoral staff to tell me of any members who wish to see me personally. I make myself readily available and can be called through my secretary. I also make myself accessible to anyone who wants to see me after any of the Sunday morning services. I stand out front shaking hands, greeting people, and discussing anything they have on their hearts.

Calvary Chapel also ministers over the airwaves, and this must account for many of those who travel long distances to fellowship here. A Nielsen survey indicated that our Sunday morning Calvary Chapel service is the most listened-to program in the area during the entire week. As of today, Calvary's outreach has included numerous radio programs, television broadcasts, and the production and distribution of audio and written resources. The missions outreach is considerable. Calvary Chapel not only supports Wycliffe Bible Translators, Campus Crusade, Missionary Aviation Fellowship, and other groups, but we donate to Third World needs. At what I felt was a leading from the Lord, we built a radio station in San Salvador and gave it to the local pastors there. We also gave money to Open Doors to purchase the ship that, in tandem with a barge, delivered one million Bibles to mainland China. Our financial commitment to missions exceeds the local expense budget by over fifty percent.

Calvary Chapel of Costa Mesa often averages hundreds of conversions a week. For years new believers were put into the highly respected Navigators' fourteen week home Bible study program. Since then, Calvary Chapel has developed its own course. As part of the course new believers can attend numerous evening Bible studies and classes taught during the week. Along with the Sunday morning and evening services, Calvary also teaches an in-depth midweek evening Bible study. On other nights of the week, thousands attend the wide variety of Bible studies and fellowship groups.

Calvary Chapel never asks for money. We avoid pressuring our members for "faith pledges" and no appeal for funds is ever made over our radio or television outreaches. Our feeling is that begging for money brings discredit to God. Financial integrity is central to this ministry. So much so that all of the staff salaries are considered low by usual standards. I limit myself and my family to a simple lifestyle while my ministry has enabled me to oversee millions of dollars. I want to be responsible to God for this money, for it is His money, not mine. I am merely a steward. This is important to me because I know that nonbelievers will be watching, and we are responsible for the way we witness to them.

I have always had problems with flashy Christian media celebrities who somehow wind up in palatial manor houses and maintain an affluent lifestyle from God's money—funds sent in by innocent, trusting, and vulnerable followers in response to high-pressure sales tactics. A personality cult is dangerous, but fiscal extravagance and dishonesty is even more dangerous. The tragedy is that all that the public sees, and in the end believes, is this image of Christians. A friend of mine calls this "Operation Caricature." These inflated public images of Christians create a cynical distrust in the non-believers, and the assumption of insincerity, naiveté, or gullibility is applied to all of us en masse. Our faith is discredited.

I believe God has blessed us at Calvary Chapel with an exceptionally loving and open fellowship. Christ told us that the world will know we are His by our love for one another. This is our predominant emphasis. And how I pray that we can consistently show the world this standard. Certainly our Lord told us that our identification marks as Christians should not only involve love, but also purity and integrity of character of the highest order. Unfortunately, the image the world most often sees of believers is that presented by those self-elected representatives who parade themselves before the public at large as holy and spiritual, while the scandals of their private lives belie this image. Their lives are as risqué as TV soap operas, which brings mocking sneers of discredit from secular observers.

We have to show the world something better than that. Yet, sadly, that numberless host of unseen Christians across the centuries who have subsisted and denied themselves on and off the mission field, living in scrupulous integrity—the George Muellers, Hudson Taylors, and C. T. Studds—doesn't even gain the slightest flicker from the media spotlight. These great lives pass by in quiet anonymity. God must help us correct these imbalances of our day and equip us to be the ambassadors of Christ we were called to be.

Let me say that in the Calvary Chapel phenomenon, I did not just walk into a church the size of an aircraft carrier and become an admiral. The church was not handed over to me, like an industrial magnate bequeathing an unworthy son some multinational enterprise. Instead, as I will share with you, I had to work from scratch and obey every new call that came from God, even when those calls seemed irrational. Behind it was blood, sweat, and tears, as well as a number of unforgettable lessons.

One of the secrets of my preparation for this work, I am convinced, was my desert years, those years of struggle. It was in this crucible that God prepared my character for the coming work. God so often makes a mockery of outward circumstances. He repudiates the impossible if we will only but believe. And believe me, my situation looked absolutely impossible at times!

CHAPTER
2

DROUGHT BEFORE THE HARVEST

*"I am not your hireling. God has called me to be a shepherd of His
Church. You had better find a replacement for me."*

These thoughts marked the major turning point in my life. I felt
God clearly speaking to my heart. And after more than seventeen
years of personal drought, seventeen years of failure in the
traditional forms of Christian ministry, I knew that this era of
confinement was coming to an end. I had come to a place where I
could no longer digest the stifling restrictive role I was required to
play. Where was the room for the Holy Spirit to work creatively
among us? In my heart, I resigned, then and there, though I held
my silence for the moment as I sat before the board of elders of the
church.

That very night the Sunday evening church service had been
unusually joyous and positive. I stepped out and took a chance. I
departed from traditional procedure and tried something that
involved everyone.

We decided to change the format from the traditional song
service, announcements, prayer, and sermon to a more informal
kind of a gathering. We were holding services in the local
American Legion Hall. So having arrived early, my wife and I
arranged the chairs in a circle rather than in a row. Rather than
using the hymnal, we worshiped the Lord in singing choruses.

Then we went into a time of prayer. And many people who had been bound were able to open up and pray. It was a very special experience for them. And then of course I shared in a more informal way from the Word of God, sitting there and teaching, more as I would within an intimate home fellowship rather than the traditional church setting.

It was electric. A lot of people got excited. But the board members had difficulty with the change of format. They were so upset they called a board meeting immediately after the service. The irony was that I had started this church. Yet the incorporating officers had not even made me an officer on the board. I was put more in the role of a hireling. Since they all had strong denominational backgrounds, they made sure that the church constitution and rules of order were virtually the same as those of a denominational church. So after seeing God move in this exciting service, they informed me that they did not want this to continue.

It seemed that our church, like so many churches, was artificially bound by extra-biblical rules and formalities, and run by men who acted as employers rather than brethren bonded together in the love of Christ. Elders were often voted into their positions because they were successful in the secular world. They had prestige or money. And so the leadership of the church was chosen by worldly standards. If they had succeeded pragmatically in business then why couldn't they help the church? It was a worldly formulation of success and had little to do with the standards of eternity. In fact, these very people can be the most inept when it comes to spiritual values and commitment because they have rooted their lives in outward success. If asked to sacrifice some of their affluence for the sake of Christ, I imagine that, like the rich young ruler, many of them would shake their heads and walk away. In our day, the Madison Avenue approach to church procedure has been sanctified.

Thus, the elders on the board used their rules of procedure to shape and confine the church to their own image. Little wonder it lacked the explosive dynamism, relevance, and love of the early Church as reported in the New Testament. It seemed that we had lost something on the way as these past twenty centuries went by. This, unfortunately, even applies to doctrinally conservative and "safe" churches. They so often follow a codified form of godliness but do not evidence the true power thereof.

As I sat before the church board that evening I kept my composure and, rather than stir up dissent, acquiesced to their request, not even seeking to defend what I had done. But in my heart burned a quiet certainty that God had called me to be a shepherd, not a hireling, or a ministerial employee on the payroll of businessmen.

I realized at that moment that this was not going to be my permanent place of ministry. It was the final move that solidified my decision to leave that rapidly growing fellowship and start all over again with the Bible study class I had in the Newport area. And the tiny fellowship at Calvary Chapel was already pressing me to come down and start my ministry with them. What was attractive in this was the opportunity to establish bylaws and articles allowing me freedom to be the shepherd responsible before God that I was called to be. I vowed in my heart that I would never again be a hireling of men.

Still, I faced uncertainty. If leaving this church was my decision alone, this costly choice would not have been nearly so nerve wracking. But naturally it involved my wife as well. I knew my decision would jolt her like an earthquake. Seventeen times she had to follow me and move to a different location. For seventeen years she had seen me work to supplement my ministry income. I had anything but a track record that would bring confidence and hope into the heart of a wife. Finally, I had worked up to a respectably sized church that was growing monthly. Only recently had we been able to purchase a beautiful new home that she loved. Now, after seventeen years of wilderness wandering, this brief oasis would once again be snatched away from her and replaced with an uncertain future. It was almost cruel. But the critical factor for me was that I was certain that God had ordained my decision to move. I had no choice but to tell her.

As usual in the churches I pastored, including the most recent, Kay formed deep emotional bonds with the people. She could not understand how I could consider leaving this blossoming fellowship that we had started, that loved us so deeply, in order to go to a small struggling church that was floundering and considering closing up shop. Not only that but officially I would be the associate pastor. I wouldn't even be the senior pastor.

"Are you sure this is the will of the Lord?" she asked me in emotional disbelief. Finally after a great deal of prayer, Kay looked me in the face. Her eyes shone like Abraham's Sarah, for she was willing to follow me anywhere. God used her to break my heart before him. This had to work. I pleaded before God with passion, though I knew God's leading was too strong for something not to be in the wind. By outward standards my move was insanity. How true that is when faith is required.

TRIALS OF FAITH

Many years before that board meeting took place, I had gone through seventeen years in the desert, a period that seemed to be one of spiritual and financial drought. And had I entertained even the most remote inkling that God might have ahead for me the scope of ministerial harvest that exists today, I would have thought it presumption, a dreamer's fantasy and nothing more. I might have laughed if you told me what lay ahead, but in derision, not in faith.

Real faith involves giving glory to God before we see any sure evidence. The Lord, I'm afraid, nailed me on this one. Years before I had pastored a church in Corona. After two years of hard work (I prayed, and I visited door to door, I printed all kinds of fliers, and tried every program in the church growth manual) our membership of twenty-five dropped to seventeen, five of whom were members of my own family! So it was necessary for me to work in a secular job in order to support our needs. God graciously opened up a job for me with Alpha Beta Market. It was a great position. Since I managed the produce department, I could go in at four in the morning and get off at two in the afternoon. That left the afternoon and evening for my ministry.

When we received word that my wife's mother died in Phoenix, we got someone to fill in at the church for us and notified the manager of the store in Corona that we were going to be gone for a couple of weeks to take care of the funeral and other family business. By the time I got back, I went in to report for work and my name wasn't on the board. I found the manager and said, "Well, I'm back now and ready to go to work." And he said, "There is a problem. You're going to have to go over and check with the union. You are behind on your dues. They said you cannot go back to work until you are all paid up."

I went over to the union to pay my back dues. They told me, "Well, you've been late so there's an assessment of a fifty dollar fine." I explained about the death in the family. They said that was too bad, but I still owed the money. Then I said that unless I was working I wouldn't even have the money to pay the fine. They replied that I could not work until I had paid the fine. And so it went, back and forth. It was a standoff, and they won.

And so without the extra income coming in we soon started to get notices that our payments were overdue. Meanwhile, the Alpha Beta Market had been wanting me to go into management. You don't have to belong to the union if you are in management. They had made an attractive and lucrative offer to me to go into market management. But their one requirement was that I no longer try to pastor a church. The president, Claude Edwards, was a former minister. They liked my work, and they liked ministers, but I would have to give up the ministry and make marketing a career.

And I thought . . . "Well, I am getting behind in my debts, and I really haven't had much success pastoring. The church *was* going down. Maybe God has called me to be a businessman. Maybe I ought to forget the ministry and go into marketing." It sounded like a fine career. And with the bills mounting up and all of the things we needed for our small children, this offer looked like a new door opening for us.

One morning I was so worried about the bills and what we were going to do that I couldn't go back to sleep. I was tossing around and worrying. I didn't want to wake up Kay, so I rolled out of bed quietly and went on out into the living room and sat there. Then I opened up the desk drawer and I got out the bills and totaled them all up. It came to four hundred and sixteen dollars. *And I thought, "Well, that's it. I can't go on any longer in the ministry. I'll just have to forget it. I'll go in today and talk to them about a marketing career."*

When the rest of the family got up, Kay fixed breakfast. Then, as I was watching our beautiful children, the phone rang. I answered the phone and when the caller asked how I was doing, I responded in a robust voice, "Oh, great! How are you doing?"

Now I made a covenant with the Lord when I went into the ministry. I told Him I would never let anybody know my financial problems. I would never ask people for money. I would never ask them to give money to the church. I would never take a second offering. I vowed at the time, "Lord, I'll never make money an issue; I will never let people know my personal needs. And I won't poor-mouth God's providence saying, 'Oh, boy, we're having such a terrible trial this month. The kids need tennis shoes...'" and so on. I wasn't going to insult my Boss by complaining about the wages.

After I told the caller that I was doing great he replied, "The Lord has been laying you on our hearts, and so we sent you a check yesterday special delivery. It should get there probably sometime today. We just thought we would let you know so you would be watching out for it." And I said, "Oh, praise the Lord! That's really wonderful of you to do that. Thank you so much." He said, "It's for four hundred and twenty-six dollars." I hung up the phone, went into the kitchen, grabbed hold of my wife, and waltzed her around the kitchen, praising God. "It's all right, honey! We'll be able to pay every bill we have! And we'll even have enough money to go out to dinner! Lord, You're so great! Thank You, Lord! Thank You! How good You are! What a blessing."

After about an hour or so, when I finally began to settle down a bit, the Lord began to speak to my heart. He said, *What are you so excited about?* And I kept burbling thank-yous to Him. He said, *How do you know they are going to send that money?* I said, "Come on, Lord, You've got to be kidding. These people have been our friends for a long time. They are good people. I trust them. They wouldn't call me up and tell me something like that unless they had sent it. Their word is good, Lord."

Then He got me. He said, *This morning when you got up, you couldn't sleep. You were moping around. Now you had My Word that I would supply your needs. And I didn't see you waltzing your wife around the kitchen. I didn't see you exuberant and praising Me. Now that you have gotten the word of man, you are all excited. Whose word do you really trust more?*

What a lesson! "Lord," I said, "I'm sorry that I didn't trust Your Word more than the word of man." If I had really trusted God at four A.M. I would have announced to Kay, "Look here at Philippians 4:19: God's going to supply all of our needs according to His riches in glory. Praise the Lord."

God was not being harsh at all, but in profound love He was teaching me a life-changing lesson. For if He is not there for us *always* our lives are sheer futility, and it is only a matter of time before the fantasy of our self sufficiency melts and we are utterly alone in the universe. Trust cannot be partial. It is all or none. Christ's lessons on faith were identical. Peter walking on water. Having the faith of a child. Simple, direct belief. Period. This lesson also prepared me for what God had ahead for me, though I would never have guessed it then. I had to learn to be faithful in the little things. I had to learn, as Abraham did, that what God has promised He is also able to perform.

My eyes had been off of God and on my problem and so it had grown bigger and bigger. But if I had gotten my eyes back on God, then the problem would have grown smaller and smaller. Abraham's faith enabled him to give glory to God before he saw any sure evidence. This was an important lesson.

A MOST UNLIKELY PROPHECY

During the era when I was still a member of a denominational church, a group of us would meet for prayer together. One of us would sit in the chair and the group would lay hands on him and pray. As I was sitting in the chair with the group praying for me, there came a word of prophecy in which the Lord said that He was changing my name. The new name He was giving me meant "Shepherd," because He was going to make me the shepherd of many flocks and the church would not be large enough to hold all of the people who would be flocking to hear the Word of God.

Then there was another prophecy that followed some years later. The discouraged group down at Calvary Chapel had met to determine whether to call me to minister or to disband. As they were praying, a word of prophecy came to them that I was going to come, that I would seek to remodel the church immediately, that I would be remodeling the platform area especially, that the church was going to be crowded to where it could not contain all of the people. The congregation would then have to move to the bluff overlooking the bay, and would eventually develop a national radio ministry, and become known around the world. A more unlikely prophecy could not have been uttered to sixteen discouraged people ready to quit and throw in the towel.

Through these experiences I have learned that God is working out a foreordained, prearranged plan. He is directing every turn and facet of my life, if I will only look to Him for guidance. Sometimes, because I do not understand the difficulty I am facing, I must look through the eyes of faith. And through faith I must realize that all things are working together for good. But then as I look back I can see that the hand of God was leading me and directing me into various things. It is so beautiful to trace His hand in my life even though sometimes He was directing me into a move that was not an easy or comfortable situation. He simply needed to teach me some lessons.

Sometimes when I moved, God was teaching me not to move without being directed. And so He let me make that move to show me the danger of going ahead without His direction. But even then I can see the hand of God as He was working out His perfect plan in my life. He knew what it would take to bring me to a complete commitment of myself to Him. And then He knew what it would take to bring me to the end of myself, where I would give up totally and completely, reckoning my old self to be dead. God knew exactly what it would take, circumstantially, to bring this transition about in my life.

God also knew the work He planned to do through me to touch the lives of others. He knew and foreordained that the work I was to accomplish for His glory would have a rippling effect until it reached around the world. Before He could work through me, He had to work *in* me, conforming me by His Spirit into His image, bringing me into the measure of the stature of fullness of Christ. Once He had accomplished His work in me, He could then do all of those things He was desiring to do through me.

I do not believe that I have fully apprehended that for which He appointed me, nor do I feel His work in my own character is complete. I still have a long way to go before I fully reflect the image of Christ! But thank God His work continues as He is changing me from glory to glory.

The Bible speaks of those who despise the days of small things. I know I was often upset in the days of preparation. Indeed I still get impatient with God. But God is preparing me for the work He has up ahead for me. God was, and still is, working in my life to condition me for that next step, whatever it might be. For Ephesians 2:10 tells us we are His "poema", His workmanship or work of art. God desires to express Himself in the lives of his people. We become the expression of God to the world, for it is through what they observe in us that they get some idea about the nature and character of the One who fashioned us, the Artist. Thus God seeks to reveal Himself through me and through all genuine believers.

As I submit to God's touch, He is able to express His poetry in and through me. This is a staggering thought, and an immense responsibility. And without His grace, it is impossible.

CHAPTER 3

As Far As The Eye Can See

In the wilderness of Galilee, where the plains meet the mountains folding in upon them, there is a beautiful but brief phenomenon. For just a few days every year, beginning one early spring morning, you can look out on what had been a plain, and see a meadow covered with a canopy of wildflowers extending as far as the eye can see—poppies, lilacs, buttercups, all radiating color and dancing in the wind. It literally happens overnight.

One morning Kay and I looked out into the California streets and on the beaches, and we beheld another radiantly colorful sight: human forms, extending as far as the eye could see. The countercultural revolution of the '60s had begun, and the new citizens were the hippies, "heads," and trippers. Their colorful outfits belied the deeper problem that they represented. God was trying to tell us something, as we looked out on that field. We faced the problem of a gap of culture and thought that stood between our generations. I was brought up in old-world piety compared to the fast-track rebellion of the hippies. How could my wife and I cross this gulf?

The Lord clearly impressed on our hearts, *Reach out in love.* Now we knew that love could never be contrived with a group as sensitive and perceptive as that one. So, to quote my wife, we saturated the air with prayers. She organized late-night prayer groups and morning prayer groups. It seemed that Kay and her friends were praying all the time. Meanwhile I prayed with elders and some church members. Before too long, we both felt a quiet change in the air, an excitement just beneath the surface.

Kay and I could feel growing inside our hearts, almost independent of our own efforts a growing burden of love and concern from God for these young people. With love would come the necessary understanding. Then we would be equipped to minister to the real needs of these estranged youths. Could this be what God had been preparing us for all these years? Were we looking at fields rich with harvest, dislocated souls ripe for almost anything from Buddha to Christ, and only waiting for the chance to commit their lives? The cultural shift had happened quickly between our generation and theirs, like the wildflowers suddenly appearing on the Galilean plains. How could we penetrate it?

Kay and I would often drive to a coffee shop in Huntington Beach and park our car. We would sit and look at those kids and pray for them. Where others seemed to be repulsed by these dirty, long-haired "freaks," we could only see the great emptiness of their hearts that caused them to turn to drugs for the answers to life that we knew only Jesus could supply. But how to reach them?

Then one day it happened. We met several youths who were hippies, yet they had a different glow on their faces. They were Christians, converted in San Francisco's Haight Ashbury district through a communal ministry called The House of Acts. They were perfect representatives of their generation, having been to all the "Human Be-Ins" in Golden Gate Park, Grateful Dead Concerts, "acid tests," Merry Pranksters events, Whole Earth Festivals, and communal experiments. They had done it all. Then one day they saw the bottom of the elevator shaft within their own souls. They glimpsed the ultimate emptiness of their pursuit, and finally called upon Christ to be the center and Lord of their lives.

We invited a couple of these youths to move into our home with us in Newport Beach. They soon moved some of their friends in as well, and it became sort of a communal house for a while. Our four kids accepted them and we began to understand their disillusionment with the church and the adult world that they called the Straight Society. They had lost all faith in any values that had preceded their generation. They took it upon themselves to find newer and higher spiritual truths and begin a revolution.

But in their rootlessness, they were supremely vulnerable. Without history they operated out of a vacuum. They were like medieval peasants going into the sophisticated center of London, naive people open to being conned by slick street sellers and card tricksters. They denied the powers of darkness while they trafficked in the occult. Yet, as C. S. Lewis observed, God is equally happy with an occultist who worships Him, as he is with a rationalist who denies His existence.

As the numbers of new believers grew, we realized that we had to find a place for these converted hippies to live. For we could not send them back to the hippie communes, knowing that they were not yet strong enough to resist the temptations of free sex and drugs that abounded there.

We started establishing Christian communal houses to hold them. The initial house elders came from the group that Kay and I had put up for a while. Their own zeal was contagious as they shared the rich truths of their newfound faith. By their zealous sharing about Jesus to those on the beaches, in the parks, and on the streets, they filled the area with the reality and truth of Christ. As we will see in detail when I discuss the lives and ministries of Greg Laurie, Jeff Johnson, Steve Mays, Mike MacIntosh, and others, this urgent and timely ministry took off like a rocket. It was irrepressible. God decided to use people whose lives had been a social engineer's nightmare. And my wife and I witnessed this miracle time and again.

OVERCOMING BARRIERS OF PREJUDICE

Ironically, the only resistance we encountered to this move of God came from the church itself, those from our midst who had grown up with church backgrounds, those from the "Straight Society." This sudden infusion of rebellious youths met predictable opposition.

Our challenge was to overcome what most churches had not, namely their insistence on respectability, conformity, and a judgmental attitude toward anything that departed from the norm.

Many of our members rallied to the challenge, feeding off the zeal of the hippie converts. But there were still some who resisted and disdained these newest members of our church who showed up with long hair, bells on the hems of their jeans, bare feet, and who otherwise looked like wildflowers in their great diffusion of dress inspired by American Indian or Asian tribal styles. It was wildly creative. But it was also threatening, especially to those with young children who did not want them emulating the hippies.

The interesting thing is how we saw love prove itself as God's adhesive force time and again. Duane Hart, a man who today is one of our elders, is a good example of the resistance many felt. He was furiously suspicious of the hippie converts. He felt that they were insincere freeloaders and manipulators who were unable to change. Never would they be able to work and support themselves.

Then one afternoon as Duane was working side-by-side with a group of hippie converts at the time we were dismantling a school building that had not been up to code he saw something that pierced his heart. These lean, muscular young men worked tirelessly as they sweat away in the summer sun pulling off the old roof tiles. Long hours went by and they never slowed down. By the end of the day, as they were scrubbing down piles of old roof tiles for use on the new structure, Duane noticed that their hands were bleeding from working so hard. And with their hands bleeding, these young men worked on into the night, singing of their newfound love for Jesus. God so convicted Duane of his judgmentalism that by the end of the day, there was not a word he could utter about them except in their defense from then on.

On another occasion, a renowned surgeon came to Calvary Chapel at the invitation of his future son-in-law, Don McClure. As Dr. Anderson told us later, he had had utter contempt for the hippie movement, and the morning he came to Calvary Chapel he was very ill at ease in the packed crowd. As much as he may have tried selectively to ignore these zealous converts, they were everywhere.

Rigid as a board, the illustrious surgeon mouthed the hymns. When it came time to read a passage of Scripture corporately, this world-renowned man had no Bible. But sure enough, someone near him did, a tall, shaggy, straggle-haired hippie. Reluctantly, condescendingly, he accepted the Bible, perhaps the way a Pharisee might take something from someone ceremonially unclean. As he opened it, he noticed that it had apparently been read with avid devotion, as Scriptures were underlined, starred, colored with felt-tip markers, and notes were scrawled in the margins. Shame and conviction flooded him. By the end of the service something in him changed.

But it really came down to my having to make a statement to men like Duane and some of our older members from straight church backgrounds. It was an issue that could have destroyed our work if we did not head it off. I told them:

"I don't want it ever said that we preach an easy kind of Christian experience at Calvary Chapel. But I also do not want to make the same mistake that the Holiness Church made thirty years ago. Without knowing it, they drove out and lost a whole generation of young people with a negative no-movie, no-dance, no-smoke gospel. Let us at Calvary not be guilty of this same mistake. Instead, let us trust God and emphasize the work of the Holy Spirit within individual lives. It is exciting and much more real and natural to allow the Spirit to dictate change. Let us never be guilty of forcing our Western Christian subculture of clean-shaven, short-hair styles or dress on anyone. We want change to come from inside out. We simply declare that drugs, striving to become a millionaire, or making sports your whole life is not where true fulfillment or ultimate meaning lies. The end of all these goals is emptiness and disappointment."

Perhaps this involves interesting symbolism, but I think that the last barrier to go in our church was the "bare feet" barrier. When we got beyond that, we were home free. The pivotal incident centered on a wide expanse of brand-new carpet that we had just put in. Those who had been inwardly protesting the hippies finally found a target upon which to vent their discontent. Dirty feet soil carpets, and these carpets cost a lot of money. Besides, who wants to see dirt marks on a brand-new carpet? They took it upon themselves, early one Sunday morning, to hang up a sign reading, *No bare feet allowed.*

For some reason I happened to reach the church earlier than usual, and was in time to take down the sign. It was sad to see division over things this trivial. It was also sad to see what really lay behind the outward demarcations of division: a we/they polarity instead of love. This time, I was the one to call the board meeting, and I would not be overwhelmed in the manner that I reported earlier. Now, not only was I on the board, but I was president of the corporation. This did not make me a dictator by any means, but it meant that I would be free to be God's man with a clear conscience, and I would not be in the position of a hireling.

Then I spoke from my heart to the board:

"In a sense it is we older established Christians who are on trial before the young people. We are the ones who told them about James 2 and 1 John 4:7. The kind of action we displayed today puts a question mark across our faith. When things like this happen we have to ask ourselves who or what it is that controls and guides our motives.

"If because of our plush carpeting we have to close the door to one young person who has bare feet, then I'm personally in favor of ripping out all the carpeting and having concrete floors.

"If because of dirty jeans we have to say to one young person, 'I am sorry, you can't come into church tonight, your jeans are too dirty,' then I am in favor of getting rid of the upholstered pews. Let's get benches or steel chairs or something we can wash off. But let's not ever, ever, close the door to anyone because of dress or the way he looks."

Calvary Chapel jumped over that last hurdle. We were ready to move ahead.

HARVEST FIELD AFTER HARVEST FIELD

Before too long, I was sending people out to plant other Calvary Chapels in other parts of California as well as across the country. Many of the people we sent out were youth extracted from the very counterculture that our "no bare feet" barrier would have prohibited. What a tragedy that would have been if we had closed the doors on them! I am sure that the flow of God's grace would have gone from a gush to a trickle if we had been that shallow.

If after all my years of struggle in God's crucible, I had not learned the lesson of following God's desires instead of man's traditional ideas, and to offer Christ's love instead of respectability and conformity, I like the salt would have been worthy of being cast upon the road to be trodden under foot. For I believe in God's eyes that I as a servant would have lost my "saltiness."

Instead, I saw the Calvary Chapel explosion of grace rise beyond my wildest dreams. Costa Mesa planted numerous Calvary Chapels, many of which have attendance that numbers in the thousands. The great work of God's design that I see here is that He has chosen as His ministers men who at one time were absolutely hopeless by society's standards. Their backgrounds embody virtually every depravity of our culture. And with almost perfect irony, the buildings that they have moved their churches into also embody almost every focal point that our society as a whole has retreated to as it has abandoned the church.

My son, Chuck, Jr., upon moving his Capo Beach Fellowship into a sizable local bowling alley observed, "We have gone to where the people are, and we have taken over their hangouts. Now when they go to our beautifully refurbished church, they are going to where they used to spend Friday and Saturday nights bowling."

Other ministries have thrived in equally unlikely settings. Raul Ries took over a Safeway store in West Covina. Don McClure took over an orange-packing house in Redlands. Mike MacIntosh first invaded one of the largest movie theaters in San Diego, then moved into a public school facility. Jeff Johnson took over one of the largest chain store buildings in the country. Steve Mays took over a similar discount house. Only Greg Laurie proved to be the one big exception: He built a massive structure designed to hold close to four thousand a service. Indeed, these were the only structures available that could contain the numbers turning out. Now Calvary Chapel churches extend to Philadelphia and upstate New York. Even on the East Coast these fellowships have grown to more than a thousand in regular attendance.

God has opened the floodgates and shown us harvest field after harvest field. We have learned that if we do not erect any barriers, and if we surrender our lives to Christ's purpose, there seems to be almost no limit to His grace. I watch this, and I stand back amazed.

A day does not pass that I do not rejoice in my heart and thank God from the very bottom of my heart. It makes every moment of my desert years worth it, and I can say with the apostle Paul, "For I reckon that the sufferings of this present time are not worthy to be compared with the glory which shall be revealed in us." I have been very fortunate to see some of these fruits in my own lifetime, especially when much greater men such as Abraham believed far greater promises and yet saw almost no sign of their fulfillment during their time on the earth.

Now I can see, looking back, that all of these moments in the wilderness of my life that had seemed so hopeless, when I felt hard pressed against the rock of despair, were worth every moment of blind struggle. God was teaching me and preparing me for His harvest by His own timetable and logistics, not mine! I could never have seen it in a million years when I was at that church of seventeen wondering whether or not God wanted me to stay in the ministry. I am thankful that His ways are not our ways, nor are His thoughts our thoughts. He can do far more through us than we would ever allow ourselves to dream.

CHAPTER
4

G R E G   L A U R I E
OPENING THE WRONG DOOR

As I responded to the ringing doorbell of our home in Newport Beach, I looked at a sight that had become quite familiar to us. A young man with long hair, bare feet, shining smile, and clear eyes had his hand outstretched as he said, "Hi, I'm Greg." He had just come from Harbor High School, which was just around the corner from our house.

He handed me a set of drawings that he said he had done that day in his art class. There, in cartoon form, were twenty-two illustrations of my message given the previous Sunday. I had spoken on the text from John 7:37 in which Jesus promised living water to the thirsty world if it would just come to Him and drink. I had shared how the thirst Jesus referred to was a spiritual thirst that everyone had for God, and pointed out the folly of trying to fill that thirst with physical things or emotional experiences. The sermon was concluded by showing that God not only fills the thirsty life, but that His Spirit will begin to gush forth out of the believer's heart and life like a river of living water.

The first picture in the series of cartoons was of a little hippie character in ecstatic joy with a fountain springing out from his heart. I was struck by Greg's perception and how he had so completely absorbed the message and so graphically portrayed its truth in the little cartoons. Greg saw my absorption in his work, and then asked in a hesitant voice, "Do you like it?" I cried back heartily, "I love it. We need to publish this."

We had been looking for a tract that would appeal to the kids on the street, one that they would not take politely, then wad up and toss away. Soon, we were off to the local quick print shop and had 10,000 copies run off. A large group of volunteers spent the afternoon cutting them into pages as others stapled them together. That night all 10,000 tracts were handed out on the streets by some of our eager kids. Demands for more came in immediately from areas where the tracts had found their way. We ultimately printed more than half a million of these tracts.

Today Greg Laurie pastors one of the largest churches in California. According to statistics gathered by the International Megachurch Research Center it is of the ten largest churches in America. It is a conservative estimate to say that fifteen thousand different people go through the doors of his church, Harvest Fellowship, every week.

As you glimpse the enormous facility approaching it along the outskirts of Riverside, California—it is reminiscent of some aeronautical assembly plant towering above the condominiums near the Kennedy Space Center—you might be surprised to hear Greg tell you that this entire ministry was a "hand-me-down" nobody else wanted. By God's grace alone it has grown into the ministry it is today. Greg is careful to tell you that it is God's church and not his.

And in Greg himself, God has turned around a life that was once bent in half by one of the worst curses of our culture, divorce. God often confounds the religious pundits of our day by using broken lives in a mighty role.

Divorce is a national sin that has marred one family after another, literally tearing this God-ordained institution in half. Children who have lived through one divorce know well enough what haunting loneliness it can create. They also know the feeling of alienation from themselves, from parents, from stepparents, and from friends.

Imagine, if you will, someone who has endured several of these parental splits and remarriages, someone who has grown up with his mother and as many as five stepfathers. No one could accuse such a person of being naive about divorce, or inexperienced in the area of loneliness and pain. Surely, this person could stand up as a representative of his entire generation and say, "I know what being from a broken family is like. I have lived through it five times." To see the grace of God overcome this crippling stigma is to triumph over one of the most evil social plagues to hit our world. Greg Laurie knows, because he is that very man.

When Christ entered Samaria, he met a woman at the well. As a Jewish rabbi, he broke tradition and shocked her by initiating conversation. He stunned her even more by offering her eternal life. And then He completely revealed the vastness of His grace by acknowledging that He was well aware of the fact that she had been "married" to five other men and the man she was living with was not her husband. Apparently she had a need for love that compulsively drove her, but she never seemed to find fulfillment.

What does this mean for us today? For people like Greg who have suffered from broken homes it is incredibly relevant. If this woman had had a son, I imagine he could cross the twenty centuries of time between them and meet eyes with Greg Laurie, his modern counterpart. With the props of time and culture removed, their emotional experiences would be very much the same. Such are the timeless effects of sin. Neither time nor custom can change them. Only grace can remove them. This is what Greg Laurie learned. It was a hard but life-saving lesson, one that he now can share with others.

THE TRAUMA

It seemed like any other school day for nine-year-old Greg. In a few minutes the bell would ring and he planned to run outside and play in New Jersey's autumn air. He liked to chase leaves about in the wind on the way home. Leaves didn't fall off trees in sunny Southern California (where he was born in 1952) as they did here in New Jersey. In fact there were hardly any seasons at all in California.

The move East had meant a big change for Greg, but he had settled into a happy and contented lifestyle. He was basking in the stability and security that he had yearned for over the years. Greg liked his latest stepfather, Oscar Laurie, whom he had come to think of as his real father, the dad he always wanted. Oscar, an intelligent and successful New York lawyer, had always shown Greg genuine kindness and affection. And when Greg needed it, this man of consistency and integrity gave him appropriate discipline. After a string of three other stepfathers Greg finally felt secure.

The bell rang and Greg fired out the school door amidst a swarm of kids and led the charge toward the street. Suddenly his frenzied excitement came to a halt. Greg spotted their family car waiting for him in front of the school. He had an unsettling feeling of dread in the pit of his stomach as if he were watching a tragically sad movie of his life. He walked slowly toward the street. The dread nearly choked him when he saw his mother inside the car. Then he noticed the boxes. Was he about to reexperience a painfully familiar scene?

Greg approached the car. "What's going on?" His mom responded matter-of-factly, "We're leaving."

"Where are we going?"

"We're going to Hawaii."

Then, through waves of fear, the movie image flickering badly, he asked, "Well, where's Dad?"

"Dad's not coming." This pronouncement was abrupt and final. The pleasant movie that had once been his life was over. And he had no idea what the next movie script of his life would be.

En route to Kennedy Airport, Greg's mother couldn't ease his tears. And during the long, agonizing flight to Hawaii, Greg reviewed in his mind the parade of faces that had stood in as his dad.

The sense of hopelessness was magnified when Greg saw the next man to enter the role of stepfather. He didn't like this new one standing at the gate at Hawaii's airport, a big rough-cut fellow. This man's face didn't have the tender honesty of Oscar's. He seemed hard, and smooth. Greg's mom, a stunning Marilyn Monroe look-alike whom men had pursued as far back as Greg could remember, stepped into the picture like a seasoned actress. The Hawaiian setting, by all outward appearances, was idyllic, but

Greg only saw ugliness. He wanted with all his heart to be back with Oscar Laurie.

They drove from the airport to an opulent house. Al, the new man in his mother's life, was rich. He even had a swimming pool. Soon, Al led them proudly down the hall to Greg's new room.

When Greg stepped into the room, he felt the mocking brunt of a bad joke. It was identical, right down to the last detail—toys, wall color, shelving, and position of the bed—to his room back in New Jersey at Oscar's house. Greg felt betrayed. Never again, he resolved in his heart, would he trust the adult world. It was a hard world of deceivers whose smiles always seemed to belie their motives.

Greg also decided at that moment that he would have to adapt to this world of hardball in order to survive. If life was just a ruthless game, he would need to be very cunning. At the doorway of his new room, Greg had passed a turning point. From then on rebellion became a way of life. He decided that the qualities of virtue, truth, and goodness, which he had once longed for, now seemed to be relegated to fairy tales, forever taunting him with false hope. Whenever they appeared, they vanished like wisps of clouds when he drew near. He had always believed in God in his heart, but God seemed to be too distant, and removed from the sad reality of day to day life.

Al let Greg do anything. He could spend the day running up and down Waikiki beach, while Al and his mom spent the day at his plush hotel bar. Alcohol was a big part of their life. Whereas Oscar had made Greg earn any money beyond his fixed allowance, permissive Al would hand out five dollar bills at the asking. On the outside, things couldn't have been better. On the inside, Greg was empty. He had everything money could buy. Unfortunately, it couldn't buy love.

It also became plain in time that the marriage between Al and Greg's mom was not made in heaven. Their fights became worse, at times loud and violent, as Greg lay awake in bed listening. It wasn't long before this marriage ended in divorce, and Greg and his mother found themselves on the plane again, headed back to Southern California.

CHANGING IDENTITIES AND PEER GROUPS

After several problem years in school, Greg entered the tenth grade. By this time he had learned how to be "cool." His goal was to hang out with the seniors. He had a quick mind, good looks, maturity, and natural charm that made him popular with almost any peer group he set his sights on. At Corona Del Mar High School, an affluent school of rich kids, button-down collars, and collegiate haircuts, for an underclassman to be accepted by the seniors was quite a feat. Yet Greg's gift at cynical mockery kept him at the center of attention. Before long he was part of the most elite senior clique, gaining him the privilege of hanging out at Senior Square, the ultimate place to be. Greg was also the cartoonist for the school paper and was always pushing the envelope as he mocked the authority structure in the school, and won the admiration of many of the students. An advantage to having little supervision at home was that he could be out all night and nobody cared. Greg and his clique of seniors often drove out to the all-night parties in Palm Springs.

But soon enough, the challenge was over. Greg saw through the clique mentality. All his hard work for acceptance had left him empty and bored. He was also struck by an ever-present sense that it wasn't really friendship that bonded his group together. They really seemed more interested in using each other for selfish ends.

Greg began to feel the same mistrust toward this peer group game as he did about the adult world. Was this conformity-minded clique of seniors any different from the adult society they would soon enter? Greg was no longer interested in their recreational drinking either. Liquor held little mystery for him. After all it had ruined his whole childhood. He had spent countless hours going in and out of bars looking for his mother.

When he reached the eleventh grade, Greg's restlessness led him to try a new identity. He would drop his clean-cut look and become a part of the drug culture. A friend persuaded Greg to transfer to Newport Harbor High School. Newport Beach was a major drug center of California, and this particular high school was famous for spearheading the countercultural drive. On Greg's first day there, he abandoned his collegiate, button-down collar look for jeans and lengthening hair. He also began experimenting with marijuana which was readily available in large quantities.

In almost no time, Greg was heavily into smoking pot with his new group of friends. Soon, he and his friends were getting stoned two times a day. It was during this time that Kay and I had our first contact with Greg, though we didn't know him at the time. On school lunch breaks he and his friends would go to a house only a few blocks from where my family lived. Kay started to notice this motley crew as they would laugh and joke on their way back to school. Clearly they were on drugs. It was at this point that the burden we felt for the youth subculture became almost intolerable. And that was when Kay and I started to pray for God to open doors for us to reach this alienated generation.

One day while working with a group of laborers dismantling a carnival, Greg was offered LSD. Greg dropped the acid while he worked, and soon was entering a new "spiritual" world where everything seemed to have hidden meanings. Insights kept flashing into his mind. He even "transcended" the fact that he almost got killed by a crane. In his mind this was a mere cosmic love tap. Greg was beginning to see eternity beneath the most ordinary things.

Greg had found a new purpose in life. He would pursue truth through LSD. As an individualist he resisted blind conformity to the hippie movement. Though he looked like any other hippie, he insisted on having his own thoughts. For that reason he did not take part in Eastern religions, nature worship, "be-ins," or communes. But Greg fully embraced the wild freedom of the time. He continued to use LSD regularly on weekends at friends' houses or in the California countryside.

At this time, Greg also began to notice a rather "uncool" group on campus. They were secure enough in their views not to care about social approval. They refused to conform to the new social revolution around them. In fact they seemed bolder than their extreme counterparts, even more than the wildest rebels who defied all morality, standards, and institutions. The heat of conflict caused them to take a highly visible stand in this wildest of high schools. At lunch they often marched across the high school campus singing hymns and handing out tracts. Greg avoided them.

They were Christians, the social lepers. The amazing thing about them was that a number had been in the dope scene much more deeply than Greg. Now they handed out tracts and smiled.

Every time Greg was handed a tract, he would look pointedly at the giver while sticking the tract into his back pocket. Greg had a drawer full of them. It seemed that every religious group had a tract in those days. For some reason he never threw them away. And now and then he would get stoned, pull them out of a drawer, read them, trying to make rhyme or reason out of the various points of view.

OPENING THE WRONG DOOR

One day Greg and a friend decided to split a mega-dose of "orange sunshine" LSD. He lay down and waited to soar into some unknown realm. Greg felt like a person with a pocket full of skeleton keys that could open one unknown door after another. The quality of the experience was strictly luck of the draw. Greg waited.

Suddenly the air seemed to ripple like water. A wave of insanity swept through him. He felt distinctly that he was losing his grasp on reality. He also became conscious of a feeling of evil—a sort of presence, if you will. Previously LSD had seemed to have a safety switch. Greg felt he could always pull out and escape if things got out of control. It was like toying with a dangerous situation without suffering the consequences, like watching a movie at one of those massive cinemadome theaters. The illusion of being in the action is so great you begin to react to the images on the screen. In an action film, you experience the thrill of being close to death without having to suffer any potential consequences.

Greg began to wonder if there really was a safety valve on LSD. He had heard of people being killed by it or going insane. Could he be sure that he could bail out? What if the insanity did not go away? A new terror flooded him.

As he felt himself going berserk, he wanted to stand in front of a mirror, perhaps to recapture who he was and remember his identity. As he stared his face started to melt. It aged hideously, then it deformed with monstrous contortions. Then something jagged ripped through him, a hideous, pealing laughter. "You're gonna die! You're gonna die!"

Greg ran outside and tried to rip his clothes off. Neighbors stared out through shuttered windows. Greg's friends grabbed him and held him. He kept thinking, *I'm in trouble, I need help. I may never get back to where I was.*

For months after that Greg felt that his brain was slightly fried. He realized that he did not want to take any more LSD. The stakes were too high.

IN THE PRESENCE OF THE LORD

One day Greg felt drawn to a gathering crowd in the school cafeteria. The fellow speaking radiated joyous hope. He was in his twenties and had flaxen hair that went down to his shoulders. He looked like he had stepped out of a Bay Area billboard advertising a concert like Big Brother and the Holding Company at Golden Gate Park. In fact, judging from his words, he had done it all. His name was Lonnie Frisbee and he was leading the youth meetings at our church, Calvary Chapel. But this speaker shared that he had come to the end of his long search; he had found the Lord. He was at Newport Harbor High that day to tell the kids why Christ (and not rock or acid) was the answer to every question they were asking. Lonnie was still in the honeymoon of his own conversion experience and was feeling the thrill of it. His joy was infectious. So was his ability to evangelize boldly. Then he said something that got Greg's attention.

Greg had been sitting, eavesdropping on this sermon. The last thing he wanted to be was a member of the "Jesus People" and become a social outcast. In the back of his mind, he knew deep down that God existed. He remembered as a small child, quietly saying prayers to Him. It was also hard to ignore that often, when he got into tight situations, he would call out to God.

In fact it wasn't long before that Greg and his friends found themselves speeding down the Pacific Coast highway late one night in the rain. They had a kilo of pot in the trunk. Suddenly the car fishtailed wildly out of control. It looked certain that they would crash and die. Greg saw the headlines in his mind, "Drug

Dealers Dead," after people found what was in the trunk. But he was never a drug dealer! They intended to smoke it all themselves! What a terrible way to go. In a quick breath Greg spoke the prayer, "Oh, God, if You get me out of this I promise I will serve You." He had done this before with God and knew that God had come through every time. But Greg would later retreat on his promises or conveniently forget them.

Now the words of Christ, spoken by the young man, suddenly cut into Greg: "You are either for Me or you are against Me." Greg never realized that. He always knew Christ was real, but he never knew that a choice of this nature existed—to be "for Him or against Him." Which was he? By not being "for Him," Greg was, in fact, in that great crowd against Christ. He had never realized you could be unwittingly against Christ. Apparently something was demanded of him, some kind of positive response. The speaker's eyes, at first mellow and loving, had become flint-like as he echoed Christ's words.

The speaker now challenged the hushed group to be "for" Jesus. Greg also noticed that a girl that he had been interested in for more than a year was one of "them," a Christian. He then began to consider what it would cost him to become a follower of Jesus Christ. He squirmed inside because he sensed he would lose his newest identity and his latest group of friends. And what about his freewheeling lifestyle? He lived for himself, for fun. And what if he was asked to make a fool of himself like these campus Christians?

But then there was another consideration eating away at Greg's mind. Because he had felt so betrayed as a child his highest allegiance had always been to find truth at any cost. Could God be the One he was really searching for? He remembered his dark and terrifying encounter with LSD. What if, one day, one of these close brushes with insanity, death, or destruction slammed the safety valve shut permanently? That would be it—the end of his life. What meaning would his life have had then? Nothing noble or good, nothing to be proud of.

Greg Laurie made an eternal decision right before the bell went off for lunchtime. He came forward, bowed his head, and that was it. He invited Jesus Christ into his life to be his Lord and Savior. He cast his lot in to be with Christ. He was "for" Christ—finally. Greg also knew he had come to the end of his search. This was it, the truth he longed for all his life.

Before Greg knew it the pretty girl whom he liked threw her arms around him. People surrounded him and patted him on the back. It was wonderful. But now the peer wars would begin. He began to wonder how long could he hide what he had done? As it turned out, not too long. It was Friday and school was almost out. That meant it was time for his old group of friends to go off into the country for the weekend and get stoned.

As was their usual routine, Greg and his friends made their way out to the wilds of nature near a national park. Someone offered Greg an acid tablet. He said no. He left them and went off alone to sit on a rock. Just as he was lighting up a pipe of marijuana, he felt the inner voice of the Holy Spirit speaking to his soul. He knew he would never smoke again. Greg Laurie, that spring day of 1970, threw away his stash as well as his pipe. It was only a day after his conversion, but it seemed like a lifetime of change had already taken place.

A FAITHFUL WITNESS

Greg went to one of the houses where he and his friends had used drugs countless times. He wanted to break the news of his conversion to them gently. In fact, he left his Bible hidden in the hedge so that he could ward off their preconceptions. Then the mother of one of his drug buddies came through the front door with a smirk on her face and the Bible in her hand. "Whose is this?" When Greg explained to his pals what had happened to him they laughed and jeered. They also expressed disappointment. To their minds, a good drug buddy was becoming a Jesus freak.

Every time Greg was put down or rejected by a different group or a friend, he realized how shallow and unsatisfying those friendships had been. He became more and more convinced that he would not sway from his newfound faith. He became almost overcome by zeal for his faith, and was soon out on the streets witnessing to people. Greg realized that following Christ was an all-or-nothing commitment as far as he was concerned. It also began to dawn on him that, for the first time in his life, he had a purpose. He no longer desired to live for himself, but to be a servant, a witness of his Lord. The old life began to peel away quickly. Within about two weeks of his conversion, Greg lost the last of his friends. Also, within that time, Greg started to go to Calvary Chapel.

Greg's first church experience as a Christian was at one of our evening services. Calvary was growing rapidly and we would soon move from a smaller building into a tent to accommodate the overflow. Greg was momentarily overwhelmed by fear before going through the door. You see, part of the toll that having five stepfathers had extracted from his soul was a very real fear of intimacy, of the vulnerability that love requires. Greg visibly trembled before going in. Finally he squeezed into a front-row seat that a friend had been holding for him, and told me later that I was one of the first adults he was willing to trust. As I taught that night, Greg's heart was set free from mistrust and suspicion to trust. In no time he was attending every function we had, immersing himself in teaching and tapes. It seemed he couldn't get enough of it.

WHAT GOD CAN DO WITH A HAND-ME-DOWN

Greg had picked up many negative "hand-me-downs" as a non-Christian youth, primarily a deep sense of personal insecurity. But God had also given him a number of positive "hand-me-downs" once he was a Christian. Greg had a tremendous desire to serve and God would soon provide many opportunities. One night, Greg went to a Bible study, and the leader did not show up. No one else had much to say, so Greg started sharing what was on his heart. The host asked him to lead the Bible study the next week and from then on. By this time Greg had been attending Calvary Chapel for a few years.

Another situation helped point Greg toward the plans God had for his life. Greg showed up at Pirates Cove at Corona Del Mar Beach, to witness one of our Calvary Chapel baptisms. By 1972 we were baptizing around nine hundred a month. Greg arrived to find no one was there. He thought he had gotten there too late. Then he saw a group of about thirty Christians singing together on the beach. He joined them, and as he did at the Bible study, Greg started sharing what was on his heart.

Soon two girls arrived and asked Greg if he was a pastor and if he could baptize them. Greg jumped up and said, "Oh, no, I'm not a pastor! I couldn't do that." But they were desperate. They felt that they had to be baptized then and there, and they were crushed that they had missed the Calvary Chapel baptism. They asked him again, and Greg assured them, "I'm not a preacher." Then he felt the voice of the Lord prompting him to honor their request.

Greg turned to the others and said, "Well, these girls need to be baptized. So let's go down to the water and do it." He walked along the beach followed by thirty-two people and thought to himself, *What have I gotten myself into?* Greg wasn't sure he had all the words right, but he did it. After it was over, two more people showed up and asked to be baptized. And Greg baptized them as well.

Afterward Greg looked up at a rock bluff above him and saw a crowd of curious onlookers. He had already performed the sacrament of baptism, but now he felt God telling him to preach. Greg stood below them and called up, "You may wonder what we are doing down here." When he was finished, a number of them gave their lives to Christ. God had just showed Greg another facet of his ministry. He had been gifted as a preacher and evangelist. As it turned out, the Calvary Chapel baptism came hours after Greg was finished.

When Greg graduated from high school, he had a very strong sense that he was to remain around Calvary Chapel and not go on to college. During that time, he continued ministering and leading Bible studies and working on graphic arts. He was around the office all the time and did numerous things to help the staff as a self-described "gopher". When I was away, he would wait anxiously for the phone to ring, for the secretary would turn those calls over to him. I often wondered what some of those callers would have done if they had known that the person counseling them on the phone was a nineteen-year-old hippie.

The next "hand-me-down" that Greg received came when he was twenty years old, almost three years after he had become a Christian. There was a Bible study in Riverside that had once drawn three hundred people, but had dropped to eighty. The problem came in finding someone to drive all the way to Riverside from Costa Mesa to lead it. My son, Chuck, Jr., had helped start and nourish it, but he felt called to start another church. After him, a string of leaders took it short-term. Then one day as the group searched desperately for a leader (and after everyone else had turned it down) they offered it to Greg.

Greg was eager to get any crumb that fell off the table, so he leaped at the opportunity. That dwindling Bible study would soon become the huge Harvest Fellowship of Riverside.

When Greg took the Bible study, attendance jumped back up to three hundred almost overnight. They shared the use of another church building, and young people flocked in. There were articles in the local papers about this phenomenon of counterculture youths turning to Christ and the dynamic and innovative leadership of Greg Laurie. He soon began traveling all over the country with evangelistic rallies.

As attendance grew, Greg felt the Lord directing them to move into their own building. About a year after joining the fellowship he found a church facility that was no longer in use, and before long I was with Greg in the realtor's office. After I wrote out the down payment, I felt the thrill of telling Greg, "You just got yourself a church."

The fellowship of three hundred jumped to five hundred at their very first service. In one year they doubled in size. That necessitated multiple services.

By 1974, Riverside Calvary Chapel (as it was then called) met in the downtown Civic Center on Sunday evenings. It had 1,500 seats. Meanwhile they expanded their church building for the morning services. But by 1980, after five years of steady growth, Greg knew that they had to build a new building. The result was the colossal structure that towers over Riverside today with the big sign "Harvest Christian Fellowship." Today, with four packed services on Sunday, they have more than 15,000 attending.

In addition to pastoring, Greg also has a passion for evangelism. The Lord has opened many great opportunities for Greg to use his gifts in recent years, from radio rallies for his nationally syndicated radio program, *A New Beginning*, to full-fledged evangelistic crusades.

In 1990, after seeing the tremendous response Greg's messages received at our Monday night Bible study, I felt the Greg should try a larger outreach. Already, an average of 100 young people were accepting Christ weekly at these meetings. That summer, we decided to hold a five-night crusade at the Pacific Amphitheater in Costa Mesa. The crusade exceeded all expectations as record crowds filled the arena and hundreds committed their lives to Christ.

So began the opening chapter of what would become Harvest Crusades, Incorporated. Within weeks, Greg and his crusade organizers received requests for outreaches from churches in various other cities in the country. Since that very first Harvest Crusade many years ago, Greg has had the opportunity to preach the gospel message to millions of people in Anaheim, California; Honolulu, Hawaii; Newcastle, Australia; and several other cities in the world. Of that number, hundreds of thousands have committed their lives to Christ.

One of the greatest evangelistic opportunities Greg had, however, took place during a radio rally in New York. A special person from Greg's past was living in nearby New Jersey—one Oscar Laurie, the only man Greg ever considered to be his father. Greg went to see Oscar and introduced him to his pretty young wife, Cathe. He also got to do something else—and this is where we see God's incredible redemptive plan. Greg was also able to introduce his father to the One who had changed his life—Jesus Christ.

Since Oscar had suffered a serious heart attack, he was beginning to weigh eternal values against temporal ones. The next day he said, "Greg, I thought about what you said last night. And I want to know what I must do to be saved and accept Jesus Christ into my life."

Greg again shared with Oscar the essence of the Gospel. Oscar replied, "I am ready to do it right now." They both knelt down and prayed. Oscar began to weep and then asked Greg if God could heal his heart. Greg blurted out, "Yes."

Then Oscar, with child-like faith, prayed for healing. In minutes, they were both convinced that God had touched him. And indeed, something had happened to Oscar both physically and spiritually. Oscar served the Lord faithfully as an elder in his church and with the Gideon Bible Society. After fifteen years of knowing and walking with God, Oscar Laurie died and is now with the Lord. Greg looks at this—along with everything else he has seen the Lord do in his life—with pure awe and gratitude.

Greg's mother, Charlene, had kidney failure later in life, requiring dialysis three times a week. She had heard Greg speak many times at the Harvest Crusades, but had never recommitted her life to Christ, though she was raised in a strong Christian home. However, shortly before her death, she returned to her spiritual roots and made a recommitment to Christ.

As we have looked at the life of Greg Laurie, we have seen the story of a man who has had five stepfathers come to discover that he had an eternal Father in heaven all along. Greg realized that God has taken his weaknesses and used even his flaws for His glory. Greg has also learned not to seek the approval of men, but of God. The huge numbers that his life has touched testify to Christ's promise of multiplying the numbers of sisters, brothers, mothers, and fathers He would add to our true family in Him.

One particular joy to him was meeting Cathe, his wife. Her appearing in Greg's life has shown God's promise that if you seek His will, He will give you the desires of your heart that are according to His will. As you recall, Greg had also been terrified of love. Now Cathe has provided him the love he always yearned for, a wholesome, loving, and stable family. And if you look at Greg and Cathe today, you learn that with God's help, it is even possible for someone from a radically unstable family background to be blessed in marriage.

When it is all said, I am not sure which is the greater gift to Greg: the harvest of his ministry, or his marriage to Cathe and their family. Either way, God has worked a miracle that keeps increasing, like the loaves and the fishes, from a few "hand-me-downs" to the feeding of thousands.

STEVE MAYS

A HEARTBEAT FROM HELL

One bleak day a hoodlum from Anaheim showed up at one of our Christian commune houses dressed in bib overalls and leathers, with a nine millimeter Beretta tucked in his back pocket. He had not bathed in three months and had literally slept in gutters while living as a fugitive from the law. He had not brushed his teeth in months and, with his neo-barbarian hairstyle, he was a sight to behold.

His name was Steve Mays and he was alienated from everybody—from his parents, who had tossed him out of their house years before, to the tough group of outlaws bikers he had been living with. He had been wanted by the authorities for what they believed to be attempted murder, and draft dodging. There was also a contract out on his life.

Steve's path to destruction seemed clearly written on the wall from the time he was a child. He had been so uncontrollable that his parents resorted to calling the police when things got out of hand. This was happening almost constantly by the time they threw him out of the house.

After a long string of bizarre events, Steve's crowning act took place one evening when he was home alone. When his parents returned, they had to shove open the front door; it had been wedged shut with towels. They discovered that their house had been made into a gigantic indoor bathtub. Water came gushing out the front door. Their son was sitting in the middle of the living room completely oblivious to the damage being done to his parents' house. He was smoking a pencil and tried to tell them about a TV show he was watching. The TV was off. He had been stoned for twenty-seven hours on yet another chemical. This time he had swallowed too much Asthmadore. He had experimented with more concoctions than you can imagine.

By the time the police arrived, his parents had gotten Steve to his room. Before his eyes his window hinges turned into toads and were apparently telling him jokes, making him laugh. When the police found out that Stephen was a member of the local high school football team, they lectured him but did not arrest him.

By noon the next day, Steve's father returned home early to have a look at his less-than-model son. This time Steve was in the kitchen fixing two place settings of milk and sandwiches. When asked who the other sandwich was for, Steve motioned to the clock on the wall and said it was for "Brad" who lived in the clock.

Not long after this episode Steve, stoned as ever (this time on LSD, hashish, and other drugs) terrorized his parents with a machete. His mother looked on in horror as Steve grimaced and paced around swinging the blade. Once he fell asleep, his bewildered parents took away the machete. To say the least, there was a considerable generation gap in the Mays' home. His father was a lab technician, a former military man and patriot. His '60s generation son had become impossible. In truth, the two had ceased communicating years before.

Looking back, Steve pinpoints one day in jr. high school when his life took a turn toward destruction. He came home from school a changed person. Everybody noticed the change, though they didn't know what had caused it. On that day, a respected authority figure, one of his teachers, had sexually molested him. It was such a terrible encounter that Steve blocked it completely from memory for years. His behavior went awry from then on. In little time, while still in jr. high school, he was smoking pot and stealing. His grades went from straight A's to D's and F's as his motivation went out the window. Life became one big game of hooky, pot, pills, speed, and beach parties. Steve was on a twisted path to destruction.

By the time Steve was in high school, his stealing had become a serious problem. He was booked four times in one week. Then by the time of the machete episode, Steve quit the high school football team (his drug antics had been getting more and more inappropriate on the football field) and became the school drug dealer. Steve and his former teammates would smoke entire "lids" in a single joint. They could get any drug they wanted and tried them all.

On one weekend mountain retreat—Steve had planned to go but for some reason couldn't—some of the football players got so high on barbiturates that they overdosed. Accidentally, their mountain cabin caught fire, but they were unconscious, too "out of it" to move. As a result, all of them were killed, and the tragedy shook the entire high school.

About this time Steve totally turned against his parents. He despised them. His hostile mood changes were further affected by changes in his body chemistry from taking "uppers" such as speed, Dexedrine, and Methamphetamine. These uppers were now keeping Steve awake three and four days straight. He was becoming increasingly paranoid because of the lack of sleep. To top it off, Steve had to find a way of releasing the fierce energy bursts that would come upon him. He would stay up all night whacking away with hammers and tools on his newest project—overhauling his sports car. When his dad came home from work he would find his son in the driveway, banging away on the car at all hours of the night. Steve was dropping out of the world fast.

His rage caused him to be in fights at school constantly. He hit one fellow thirty-one times in the face. He cut off another guy's finger. By the time his orders to appear before the draft board came, Steve defiantly burned his draft card and went on the road. As far as Steve's parents were concerned, the only place left for him to go was out the front door. They had an incorrigible rebel on their hands who was beyond hope.

A HEARTBEAT FROM HELL

Steve's new place of residence was in a section of Orange County known as Garden Grove, in the hangout of a motorcycle gang. Steve was able to stay as long as he applied his mechanical talents to motorcycle body work. But he soon found out that his fellow tenants were fierce masters. If his parents had been unloving or alienating at times, these new housemates were positively demonic. Steve discovered a terror that he never would have dreamed existed back on the old homestead. He found himself trapped in a spiritual environment that most people don't know about, or would never want to know about.

The motorcycle gang members were in their mid-thirties, twice Steve's age. They also carried guns and were heavily involved in crime and drug-dealing. As bad as Steve was, he was innocent compared to them. Another thing that set Steve apart was his choice of drug. This might seem like a minor point, but it made all the difference in their social world. They were into reds or "downers," while Steve was maniacally on "uppers." His frenetic binges got on the nerves of a few of them. One of them especially had it in for Steve and he began scaring him more and more with his guns. It seemed that the increasingly violent and terrifying incidents were rapidly becoming nothing more than a sadistic game.

I will let Steve Mays recount this era, as he has done often when giving his testimony:

"One night a motorcycle was tipped over. They woke up and said I did it. I would stay up all through the night and separate bolts and nuts and put them in absolute order. Then I would dump them all out on the floor and work through this same ritual again. That was how stoned I was. I would take the twenty Dexies and crush them, I would add an Excedrin, a vitamin, and put it all in a horse pill and swallow it with coffee. I would get so wired my mind would just fry.

"So they woke me up early one morning after my binge was over. They said that I had rolled the bike over. I told them I didn't touch it.

"The guy who had it in for me reached for something. Then I saw the blue barrels of a twelve-gauge double barreled shotgun. He told me to open my mouth while the others held me and helped shove it in my mouth. Then I said, 'That isn't loaded, is it?' They pulled it out, pointed at the pillow next to my ear, and pulled the trigger. It blew pillow feathers all over the place. Then they stuck the shotgun back in my mouth and smoke began to come out. I thought I was going to die. My paranoia really began to grow from then on. That's when another guy living there gave me his gun to protect myself. It was then that I started carrying a gun. I would have to stay awake all night to make sure that I wouldn't die, living in the same house with a guy who wanted to kill me.

"Soon after that I was out in the backyard working on my motorcycle. He came out in the yard with a thirty-eight pistol. I was sitting on a gasoline can as a chair, while I worked on the cycle. He shot three rounds into the bottom of the can. He missed me, and it was just by a miracle that the gas can did not blow up with me on it."

Still, Steve did not leave the house. He learned the lifestyle of his older mentors and became freewheeling with his new pistol. As the house began to sell more and more dope, Steve began to deal more. A girl who came by to get dope wanted to buy it from another guy and not Steve. This infuriated him, so when she walked away, he fired his gun at her. But he was too stoned to hit her. The bullets flew over her head. Then the rage mounted. He now wanted to kill something, anything. The target became a cat.

"I shot this alley cat with a P-38. It just smiled at me after I shot it. I felt sickened inside for doing it, but I just kept my feelings inside. From that point on, every place I went there was a cat. I think that was the closest I came to being demon-possessed."

A member of the gang told Steve that someone had taken a contract out on him. Steve had been working on three motorcycles that he used, a shovel-headed Harley Davidson 1200 cc Hog, a '49 Indian, and a Trike. But where do you go when you don't even know who has the contract out on you? Instead of running, Steve got a shotgun with a twelve-inch barrel and a pistol handle, and began practicing with it in the garden.

But one evening, at a time when Steve wasn't suspecting anything, his old enemy who lived in the house pulled out a thirty-eight pistol and pointed it at Steve, and said, "I hate you. There's a contract out on your head, and I may as well collect on it as anybody else." Steve heard an explosion and felt searing pain, like white-hot wrought iron, tearing the calf of his leg. He passed out.

A day or so later he woke up laying out in some field. He had been given a large dose of reds to knock him out. He discovered cloth rags in the hole in his leg. The muscles of his calf had been blown out. The blood had dried, and the pain was excruciating as he pulled the rags out. He knew that he could not go to a hospital because the authorities had a warrant out for him. Nor could he go home, because his parents (whom he had wanted to kill) would call the authorities.

Incredibly Steve had only one place to turn, the same house where he was shot. Several gang members took him to the home of a nurse he knew, a neighbor of his parents. To silence her, he threatened to kill her. She cleaned out the scabs and dried blood. By the third visit to her, she finally got the courage to call Steve's parents. Steve's mother called the FBI while he was still getting his leg cleaned. When Steve and several members of the gang pulled away from the house in their car, they sensed something was up.

Steve describes what looked liked a hopeless predicament:

"I hadn't been home in years. So the authorities used my parents' house as a stakeout location. As we headed out of the nurse's house, I noticed a red Mustang making a U-turn. For once we weren't armed and had no dope. Two guys were in the front seat, and I was in the back. The pursuit began.

"As we slowed down for a red light, the Mustang ran into the rear of our car, sending us careening into the middle of the intersection where three other cop cars suddenly wedged into us. They surrounded us with rifles and shotguns and shouted, "If you move, you're dead!" They pulled me out of the backseat and kicked my legs apart in order to search me. I can still remember the gun being held to my head and the shotguns aimed at us. "Once again I thought for sure that I was going to die. Before I knew it, the officers had slammed my face against the hood of my car, which in the 100-degree summer heat amplified the scorching pain.

Then they handcuffed my ankles and my hands and threw me into the back of their car.

"The authorities came and also examined my leg. They realized they had me for draft evasion and thought they had apprehended me—the right suspect for shooting an old lady. I had been accused of shooting this lady during a robbery. She had told the authorities she returned fire with a rifle and hit the suspect with a .22-caliber bullet. Fortunately, it was clear I had been shot by a .38-caliber bullet.

"Then the authorities let me go! All I was required to do was report to the draft board, which I did. To my surprise they also released me, not wanting to send me to Vietnam because of my gunshot wound. I never understood why either agency let me go. However, it is clear to me today that God was beginning to move in my life."

Even though being released by the authorities was a miracle, to a gang member it is probably the worst thing that could happen. To be the first one released normally meant you sold out your companions to secure your own freedom. Thus, the gang members were convinced that Steve had betrayed them. Therefore, they kicked Steve out of the gang house. Now Steve had no place to live. He began sleeping in gutters. Still suffering from drug-induced paranoia, he was now plagued with the possibility of being found, beaten up, or shot again, on the streets. So he continued living as an outlaw.

MANSION MESSIAH SOUNDS GOOD

"I was sleeping in the gutter one day and a couple by the name of Shirley and Henry came out to their car, which was parked near me as I lay in the gutter. They picked me up and took me inside their house, gave me a shower, fed me. She told me she saw Jesus in my eyes. Then she called three different organizations and one of those was the Mansion Messiah House of Calvary Chapel. She asked which one I would like to go to. I replied, 'I don't know, Mansion Messiah sounds good.'

"They took me over to Mansion Messiah. I walked in with my gun stuck in the back of my pants. Immediately, this little squirt named Orville looked right in my eyes and said, 'Do you know Jesus?' And I said no. And then he said, 'Bow your head, we're going to ask Jesus into your heart.' And I said the sinner's prayer after him. That happened without anyone explaining the Gospel to me.

"Everything suddenly clicked. God just grabbed me, reached in and burned in my heart. It was the most incredible power I have ever experienced in my life. It was a tremendous burning sensation of an inner witness. It was something of the awesomeness of God's love. I can't even express it.

"At that moment God delivered me from drugs. I flushed ten thousand dollars' worth of drugs down the toilet that day. I have never touched any drugs since that time. I also threw my gun away in the ocean. The residents of Mansion Messiah buried my clothes, they smelled so bad. From then on, I started singing Christian songs by myself when I was just walking down the street.

"For the first time in years, I telephoned my mom that same day and told her that I had accepted Jesus Christ. As I was describing what had happened to me, she said, 'Anything that can save you, I want it right now.' She came to the Lord over the phone. Then I witnessed to my dad and he said, 'I don't want to hear about it. I want to see it.' So for the next few years, I never witnessed to him, I just lived a changed life. But when it looked like he was dying in the hospital of cancer, I told him I could no longer hold back from discussing Christ with him. His eternal destiny was at stake. It was then, finally, that he accepted the Lord. Those long years that my parents and I never had a relationship have been replaced by a healed relationship that we share together. In all these changes surrounding my life, it is hard to say what the greatest miracle is. Even my brother, Gary, came to know the Lord along with his wife, Judy."

Steve Mays frequently shares God has taken him from the "guttermost" to be used to the uttermost:

"It became a family joke when an aunt of mine, who was a Christian, would remind my parents of a prophecy about my life during some of my worst high school years. She said flatly that one day I would be a preacher. Now the impossible has happened. Not only am I, Steve Mays, a Christian, but I am a pastor as well. And who would have ever dreamed, during my most demonic years, that one day I would be pastoring a church that my own parents and brother would attend!"

CROSSING THE DESERT TO THE OASIS

But this blossoming ministry of Steve's did not happen overnight. In fact, more than once, it looked as though Steve would never even pastor a church.

In 1971 he became a resident of Mansion Messiah for a year, then switched over to another communal house for another year. It was then that Steve felt God's voice clearly tell him that he had been called to the ministry. But he had years of cobwebs to clear out of his head from drugs and general rebellion. Christian character had to be formed in Steve in a slow and costly way. There is no shortcut in this process.

Steve's first position that involved the responsibility of spiritual leadership came after he had spent over two years in two of our Costa Mesa houses. One day Steve felt led to go out to the California desert area of Victorville and start a Christian commune. He called my brother Paul and soon learned that they had been praying for someone to come out and start a commune.

Steve's desire was granted. Before too long, a house in Victorville was started with a total of thirty residents. Four Calvary Chapel pastors came out of its ministry. Steve also started a coffeehouse. Around this time, he started calling me weekly to bug me about giving him the go-ahead to start a church. But I did not feel he was ready. Indeed, when I finally did call him to come back to meet me one day in Costa Mesa, Steve was fully expecting me to ask him to come on our staff. He was crushed when I advised him to start a gardening business. He returned to the Victorville commune devastated. In fact, he felt that after all his years of reckless abandon and sin, the only plan God had in store for his life was to punish him out on the desert. And, indeed, that was where he was living at the time, in the midst of his own desert experience.

But those desert years were very important in the Spirit's preparation of Steve for the ministry that God had in mind for him. Steve had a set of my commentary tapes on the whole Bible and he began to listen to several of them each day. These tapes triggered his desire to know the Bible. His thirst for God's Word became almost insatiable and he began to build his own library of Bible commentaries which today has become one of the most extensive of any minister I know. In the desert, Steve began to experience his inner spirit being satisfied by the Living Water.

One day in Victorville, as Steve was serving the Lord, an amazing thing happened. A pretty blonde girl passed right in front of Steve's eyes. She had long hair past her waist, with a flower by her ear. Steve recalls:

"I couldn't help but take a second look! Her face was aglow with the love of Jesus Christ. Her name was Gail. Then I heard the most bizarre thing. It was a voice that said, "This is your wife." I remember responding in my heart, "Satan, get thee behind me!"

Yet Steve knew that it was God speaking to him and that He had laid this woman upon his heart. Steve was stunned and speechless. Yet Gail was only visiting this Christian house. Her home was in Orange County.

That evening, Steve immediately began to question exactly what God was speaking to him. He knew there was something special about Gail. Deciding to search the Scriptures for answers, he opened his Bible and the pages fell open to Proverbs 18. The passage Steve immediately saw was Proverbs 18:22: "He who finds a wife finds a good thing and obtains favor from the LORD."

Steve was still doubtful. He had been hurt by previous relationships and decided to put God to the test. He prayed, "OK, Lord, if I call her and it just happens to be her birthday [as he had heard] and if no one is celebrating with her and in fact she is weeping over this, then I will believe."

Steve doubtfully called her. To his amazement, the situation played out exactly as he had asked. He said to her, "Do you want to come out to Victorville and spend time together?" Gail's response was, "I will be there within a couple of hours." And she left for Victorville immediately.

That evening they went out to dinner. Gail remembers thinking that Steve was too poor to eat as he ordered just a small bowl of soup, but in fact Steve was too nervous to eat. Gail thought he was going to invite her to stay in Victorville and help with the commune as one of the sisters in charge of the women. Instead, Steve proposed to her! To his shock, she accepted immediately. Steve recollects:

"The next day I called my mother and told her I was getting married. She was shocked, to say the least. She said, "Stephen, I just talked with you a week ago."

"I know, Mom, but God has really spoken to my heart."

"Stephen, what is her name?"

"Gail," I said.

"And her last name?"

"Mom, I didn't ask her! I will call her and ask her right away!"

"My poor mother probably wondered if I was back on drugs again."

In one week, Steve and Gail were married, and my brother, Paul, performed the ceremony.

Not long after that I called Steve to his first church—in the desert. My son had started a church at Twentynine Palms and had moved on to Yuba City to start a ministry there. This was the last place Steve wanted to go. But he showed up, ponytail and all, to the desert community of a military base. Two years later, absolutely broken, he and Gail showed up at the Calvary Chapel Costa Mesa parking lot to find me. In silence, Steve dropped the keys to the church into my palm. The church had divided and finally closed. Steve thought that it was all over as far as being in the pastorate was concerned.

I immediately offered Steve the directorship of half of our Costa Mesa communal houses, including the House of Psalms, where he and Gail lived for seven years. Gail was heartbroken, because she was leaving a three-bedroom house to share a cramped house with forty other people. Their new kitchen became the meeting hall, so Gail did her dishwashing in the bathtub. But they also saw over a thousand changed lives pass through those communal houses. It was a sacrifice that had eternal rewards.

After those seven years Steve started a church in Buena Park, now known as Calvary Chapel of Cypress. Then, after two years, he was told by the Lord to leave and submit to another pastor. So for two years he was an assistant pastor at Hosanna Calvary Chapel of Bellflower. He had somehow lost his priorities, he felt, and was now rededicating his life to the Lord. But he was also afraid that he just wasn't material to be a senior pastor. He had tried this twice and failed. But God was not finished with Steve yet, a fact He would communicate to Steve in a beautiful and unique way, and then back it up circumstantially.

Steve had reached a point of despair in which he had finally given up ever having a church of his own. His final stipulation to the Lord was: "Chuck Smith is going to have to call me to the position." Then he went on a long overdue vacation.

As Steve was fishing, he started talking to the Lord and asking for some kind of sign: "If I am ever going to pastor again, Lord, I am going to have to catch a fish before this hook leaves the water." Steve started to reel his line in while the hook glinted under the surface. Just as the hook was about to break through the top of the water, Steve's eyes welled up with tears. No fish would bite it now, it was too late. Just as it was coming out of the water a tiny fish bit the hook. That tiny fish meant more to Steve than any five-pound bass. For Steve detected the voice of God speaking to his soul, confirming his request for a sign, and then saying, In a little moment, I will speak to you again.

When Steve returned from his vacation, he got the message that he was to call me or Don McClure. He was told over the phone that there had been a meeting of all the senior pastors at the last conference and that when the newly available position of pastor of the South Bay Calvary Chapel was discussed, his name was unanimously recommended. Steve was so excited he almost passed out.

Steve Mays got his church, and the board of senior pastors and I were the ones to recommend it. In 1980 he walked onto the premises of his new church. And Steve got more confirmation from the Lord. Suddenly in the sky he saw a Goodyear Blimp. At that moment he heard the Lord speak to his heart, It's going to be a good year.

Then Steve told the Lord that the entire board of elders would have to resign so he could start from scratch.

That is exactly what happened. In 1980 Calvary Chapel of South Bay numbered 50 and occupied 1,500 square feet. Within a few years they moved to a bigger facility nearby, 15,000 square feet that they remodeled for $300,000 dollars. By then the Goodyear people had heard the often told story of Steve's glimpsing the Goodyear Blimp, so they took him up for a free ride.

It was not only a good year, but they have all been good years. The glorious harvest has come upon Steve Mays' ministry, and that church of only 110 per Sunday has grown to over six thousand.

Meanwhile the years that the powers of hell stole from Steve have been restored in a stunning way. The former dropout and quitter, as his high school coach once called him, was recently the key speaker at the Anaheim Sports Banquet. Steve's old coach gave him his letterman's jacket after seventeen years, and Steve addressed the entire football team about not giving up. Steve, who once loved baseball and who had a batting average of .450 in high school, got the chance recently to talk to the Los Angeles Dodgers, addressing the team in Dodger Stadium, thanks to an invitation from his friend John Weirhaus and Victory Ministry.

Steve and Gail have two healthy children, blue-eyed blondes who don't have any sign of Steve's scars. They excel in sports, academics, and loving obedience. And Gail has a home she can be proud of, much nicer than the one she had to abandon at Twentynine Palms.

Steve now sees that God has flooded his life with almost more grace than he can contain. He is a living testimony. To use his own words, "By the grace of God, I have not only regained what Satan ripped off, but I have been given a greater abundance of positive effects than all the evil I heaped up in the past."

We have seen a life literally go from the gutter to grace. The only thing Steve carries on his body to remind him of his former years is that painful scar on his leg. To this day, it still hurts. It serves as a reminder to teach Steve gratitude. It also helps him to never forget the pit from which he came, and the greatness of God's grace that brought him out of that pit.

Zechariah speaks of the days when Zerubbabel had laid the foundations for the rebuilding of the new Temple as "the despised days of small things." Steve, for a time, was caught in that desire to build the walls before the foundation was laid. In this he learned that it is vitally important not to build out of sequence, but to dig deep and lay the foundation on the Rock.

CHAPTER
6

JON COURSON
FIRE & RAIN

Jon Courson stood on the banks of Yale Creek in the Applegate Valley of Oregon. This husky fellow was silhouetted against the vibrant green all around him, as his thick mane of red hair shone in the summer sun. Before him stood the members of a colony of young people who had built a treehouse community in the Applegate hills. They were standing in the nude in the middle of the river waiting to be baptized and resembled aging nature children as their long hair blew and glinted in the sunshine.

Jon felt conflict over whether or not to make an issue over their nudity. He went with his gut sense, and decided to overlook it. This group before him had for years been a community of pot-growers whose treehouse commune was on a large tract of land they owned. Their marijuana harvests had made large proceeds for them while their "Nirvana Community" had looked for enlightenment through Eastern yoga and native American shamanism. But the bubble of their dream had burst. Just when they had built their ideal community, a gaping vacuum appeared within their hearts. This huge utopian experiment had not satisfied their souls.

Then in the late seventies Jon Courson came to this wilderness with his wife, Terry. Soon, gently, this broad-shouldered Christian neighbor started to tell the treehouse-dwellers about the love of Christ as he met them by a beautiful stream. He would run his hands through the water and talk about his faith. They saw a strength and a hope shining in his eyes, a joy, that they had not found. Jon seemed to have no need for drugs or any other kicks. He was as solid to them as a California redwood. But his strength did not come from himself, but from the One whom he continually told them about.

With waves of mounting inner joy, Jon baptized each one of them in the name of Christ. They stood on the banks dripping and smiling ear to ear. That evening they would gather up all their marijuana and burn it in a huge bonfire.

Jon was overseeing building a church from scratch in a region of Oregon so sparsely populated that no demographically-oriented church planner would ever give the effort a chance. Applegate was a region containing verdant mountains, forests, and clear rivers with a widespread population of fewer than a thousand.

It was near the northern California border, and from there to Eureka, California, tribes of pot-growers tilled their crops, some of them with semi-automatic rifles. The leader of this community, once notorious, was now giving up his rich lifestyle to follow Christ.

This was the first of five waves of pot-growing converts in the Applegate Valley. This particular group became tree-planters in their Oregon community. One of their members eventually became the pastor of a Calvary Chapel church in the state of Washington. Another became a pastor under Jon.

Recently I got a letter from a spin-off fellowship from Jon's church in Ashland, Oregon, that now has 1,000 members. The letter described the impact when a major commune of pot-growers became Christians. A few of them went to the Ashland Christian Fellowship where they got some of my Bible-teaching tapes, and began to play them while they worked on their marijuana harvests. One day they asked themselves, "Is what we are doing right?" Soon after that they accepted Christ en masse, burned their pot, joined the fellowship, and started a natural food business called Maranatha Nuts that made various kinds of natural foods. Theirs has become the most successful business in the region. When I read their letter at Calvary Chapel Costa Mesa, there was extended applause.

When Jon first came to Oregon, he had only five couples attending his fellowship. He had left a thriving Calvary Chapel that he and his brother had started in San Jose. But he was certain the hand of God was directing his move.

Before Jon moved to Oregon, there were two prophetic visions about the coming harvest. The first vision was of fire descending on Applegate Valley and then spreading beyond. The second vision of massive thunderheads pouring out rain foresaw the end of Oregon's long drought. And a further message was that God's grace would be released when the first rains came. Jon was reluctant to accept these visions as prophecies and was by no means sure he would leave San Jose for Oregon. Interestingly, the day Jon began his first Sunday service there, the rains came flooding down. He also sensed in his heart that God's grace was being released.

Today Applegate, Oregon, is still a small rural community, but its Calvary Chapel fellowship, Applegate Christian Fellowship, is known throughout the region. Its church membership of several thousand comes from many surrounding communities. They are now meeting in a large church facility of 40,000 square feet that they built together. Vast beams run along the ceiling and huge plate-glass windows look out into the beautiful valley. In the summer, they meet in a large grass-covered outdoor amphitheater near the main church building. Both structures and a vast parking lot sit on their forty acres. The large outdoor amphitheater is bordered by flowers and surrounded by an excellent sound system. I had the pleasure of dedicating the new church building and large pictures of the event headlined local papers.

Jon has experienced the fire and the rain of this harvest. He will tell you flatly that it is a miracle. Indeed, 35 other spin-off Calvary Chapels have come out of this one enormous church. John Peterson went to Grants Pass initially while Guy Gray went to Medford. Soon others followed. They had witnessed the huge crowds assembling in Cantrall Buckley Park to hear Jon preach in the summer and fall months of 1978 and 1979. Jon is often reminded of that early vision of fire descending on Applegate Valley and spreading outward to other communities.

Jon has also learned that there is a purifying aspect to fire in biblical imagery in which one's work for God is tested in the fire. And all hay and stubble is burned leaving only the enduring works of gold and precious gems. Jon has also experienced these waves of fire, during times of testing, and has seen his church rebuilt on stronger foundations following each wave.

PIONEERING INTO NEW TERRITORIES

A little more than twenty years ago, Calvary Chapel fellowships started spreading out beyond California and opening up in various parts of the country. Almost without exception, those who pioneered these churches, like Jon Courson, spent time at Costa Mesa learning and fellowshiping with us. At the right time each would feel the nudge from God and move out. As can happen, there are some who are not of our fellowship who have used our name for their own ends. Now and then we hear reports of wild activities that in no way reflect our beliefs. We believe in the church-building approach that only humility and the love of Christ can bring, not modern extravaganzas or money collection schemes.

Calvary Chapel pioneers came from a diverse range of backgrounds. Jon Courson was a student at Biola University in nearby La Mirada, California, when he started attending Calvary Chapel. Unlike some of our ministers with more sensational and bizarre backgrounds, Jon represented the epitome of normalcy, adjustment, and graceful conformity. He stood out as America's ideal son of moral virtue and hard work when contrasted with some of the wild rebels among us. And without a doubt, Jon has added a significant piece to the mosaic that God is building through Calvary Chapel's ministries. The picture would be incomplete without his "type." He further adds to the design that God uses all people to serve Him: from the outrageous, like Steve Mays and Mike MacIntosh, to those who represent the unscathed center of the American heartland.

Jon Courson and George Markey, a big strapping mid-Western farm boy who pioneered a Calvary Chapel in his rural farm community, could probably walk comfortably into early America. They are our nation's Johnny Appleseeds and Paul Bunyans, the carryovers from former eras of national innocence and purity. They are products of old American virtues, a fact that can be evidenced on their beaming faces. Their handsome faces radiate virile strength tempered by gentle self-control. I am afraid they are a vanishing breed of men. Replacing them is what some call "the new male."

And this brings me to a subject that greatly burdens me. Permit me, if you will, to digress for a moment over an issue that is critical to our time. Our world and its media have turned against the old traditional order of men and women, as it applauds the new androgynous male and female roles.

The new male has shunned what for time immemorial has been recognized as healthy masculinity for a new "liberated" blending of added feminine traits. This is nothing new. It is the scale on which this transition is happening that bothers me. As someone said, they have become "women-thinking men," or "touchy/feely men". They are anything but equipped to head a household or sire a healthy family. Rather, they herald the age of single-parent families and confused sex role models as they sport the latest markings of their newfound freedoms. They are men who wear single earrings, fellows with unisex haircuts who have brazenly strayed into the women's side of the department store. And they have done it with defiant pride, encouraged by sneering anti-male women who themselves have trampled underfoot any wholesome femininity that they might have had for a brash, defiant, pseudo-masculine hardness.

Meanwhile the new touchy/feely men have joined the shrill voices in protest against any reminder of the once-common strong traditional male. This gale of radical dissent can be heard on almost any college campus, headed by the lesbian and feminist coalitions and assorted anti-traditional and leftist minorities and causes. They would put traditional America, and all historical records of it through the shredder if they could. The New World Order they espouse is collectivist, amoral, anti-family, anti-American, and anti-Christian. The ideal of a biblical man who is strong and not vacillating or weak is anathema to them. An intimidated "wimp" is far less threatening.

This group postures as broad-minded and non-judgmental—and so they are as long as you happen to be "gay," feminist, liberal, liberationist, socialist, or Marxist. However, if you are a Christian, especially a "traditional" white male, then you are targeted, and they can employ the full sanction of "enlightened" society to hurl any judgments at you they wish with total impunity. The uncommitted middle-of-the-roaders, who are fearful of being singled out, will contort wildly to avoid having any loaded accusations hurled at them. The use of insulting terms like "sexist" and "racist" will bring all sorts of people into line. A football player or a college professor will wilt before a group of wild-eyed feminists that has labeled them "sexist." Indeed, intimidated people have given this ugly and bent coalition unilateral power to judge and define them at whim.

An agenda of social castration has almost been fully consummated, and the results are sordid. A college president will perform delicate pirouettes to avoid speaking in non-inclusive language at commencement exercises so he won't offend various feminists and minorities present. The word "person" is suddenly affixed to every other word. It is a perfect instance of what Orwell called news speak. Few have the courage to stand against this ugly trend headed by a shrill-voiced minority who would have barely spoken above a whisper fifty years ago.

In all of this, the atmosphere between the sexes has become contentious, cynical, and mistrusting. Individual "rights" are so on the forefront that the bonding of men and women in marriage is close to an impossibility. Divorce statistics bear this out.

Have you noticed that men and women are hardly falling in love anymore? This causes the homosexual groups to gloat privately. In today's atmosphere it is little wonder that this is so when you consider that modern society resembles what Paul describes in his second letter to Timothy: The social rebellion has truly been incredible.

Jon Courson felt called by God to stand against the beginnings of this social rebellion by being a role model. At the time, the latest anarchy was the hippie movement of the late '60s.

A NORMAL APPLE PIE YOUTH

Jon had fully distinguished himself as an outstanding athlete and scholar by the time he was in high school. He was senior class president and captain of the football team. By the time of his graduation, his class honored him with three awards, an unprecedented action. He was voted most popular, best personality, and best outlook on life. He was also winner of the Principal's Cup as the outstanding graduate of his high school. Finally, Jon won the District Superintendent's Cup as the outstanding graduate for his whole district in Northern California.

As President of the Baptist Youth of Northern California, Jon already had an active speaking ministry during high school. He addressed youth retreats, camps, and church groups. As a hero figure, Jon's life proclaimed the virtue of godly obedient living over and above the rebellion so glamorized by America's youth. Here was a healthy and handsome honor society student and football captain who managed to have fun and fulfillment without having to resort to drugs and corrupting influences. His life was saying, "You don't have to be a rebel to be fulfilled or happy."

Consistent with Jon's disciplined life, he received a full athletic scholarship to Biola University, a Christian school. This broad-shouldered, big-armed young man held his high school conference record in the discus. His performance improved in college to the point where he ranked eighth nationally in the NAIA college division. He had also begun riding his ten-speed bicycle out to Calvary Chapel on weekends, spending Saturday nights sleeping on the bathroom floor. This we learned later.

Jon's zeal was hard to miss. Yet there were things happening inside him that would direct his life on an unexpected course. Jon's well-calculated path of conformity and honorable good deeds had some problems. He was a popular man on campus who bathed in all the outward rewards of being a do-gooder and role model. He was the cream of the crop of Baptist youth and fully expected to walk into a well-appointed ministry. The mechanism had already been set in motion.

The problem was that this young zealot was beginning to be confronted with issues that required hard and costly decisions. He was also having an intense new encounter with God. And that can be dangerous and costly to one's plans, designs, and ambitions. Among other things, Jon was coming to understand how greatly his "good" actions fell short of the perfection of God's standards. Our greatest efforts are cheap imitations of His righteousness.

Jon was also working through some theological questions. Back then, some of Jon's professors were suspicious of Calvary Chapel and delivered subtle warnings that we should be avoided. There was a little too much going on out here as far as they were concerned. They wondered aloud if the seeming revival was a signal of cultic activity.

Jon was not persuaded by his professors. He felt instead that God was being kept in a box by the academic theologizing of history. He also felt the constraints of spiritual legalism. A tight and regimented system of piety quenched him. He felt he was participating "in a form of godliness but denying the power thereof". He felt trapped and hemmed in by a system that discouraged encounters with God of the sort reported in the Bible. Jon was studying the vitality of the early Church in the book of Acts, with its sense of reality and mission and power, and wondered why modern Christianity had to settle for a diminished and powerless faith. Had God changed through history? Had He mellowed into deism? The powerful early Church seemed relegated to ancient history. It stood before Jon teasingly, as if he were on the outside looking in, like watching a banquet in an exclusive club through a window.

Jon came to Calvary Chapel in the fall of 1972. He has often shared his initial reaction. "All of a sudden I was gripped with this incredible certainty that all that I had been studying in the classroom about the book of Acts was happening before my very eyes. It was suddenly real and was truly happening today. I was astonished over the possibility that I could find New Testament reality today. It revolutionized my life. The spiritual dryness inside of me suddenly flooded with restored hope and vitality."

Unlike most of our Calvary Chapel pastors, Jon grew up in a strong Christian home. But he had to battle things that his peers were unaware of, namely, that unending seduction of good works and legalism that can stand in the path of so many Christians. It can make one lose sight of the miracle of God's grace so easily, and cause people to follow tight rules while judging all others ungraciously in the process. This legalistic trap vexes Christians time and again. They end up spiritually paralyzed, joyless, and without love. Certainly without the love of God, Jon could not have seen those waves of conversions in Applegate Valley.

A key moment of reckoning for Jon came when he was addressing hundreds of youth. All of a sudden God pointed to Jon's heart and said, *You don't care about these kids at all. You are expounding truth with absolutely no love for them. You have no love for them at all. And that is a lie.* For two days after that Jon drove around in his surfing van. He told God that if he was not given love to minister with, he would abandon his plans of going into the ministry.

By Jon's graduation, he had told the Baptist conference that he wanted to work with Calvary Chapel. Immediately, their doors of opportunity slammed in his face. Calvary was still very much an emerging and misunderstood ministry. "Non-denominational" can be a term that can create suspicion in denominational churches. After Jon's graduation, he taught for a year at our Twin Peaks conference center in the mountains above San Bernardino. And a year or so after that, he and his wife, Terry, were off to Oregon. But, completely unbeknown to him, a vicious trial lay ahead of this stouthearted fellow.

TRIALS BY FIRE

Jon could have been accused of having it easy. He did not come from a family of five stepfathers like Greg Laurie, or a family that was coolly rejecting, like Steve Mays. Jon Courson's family was the embodiment of American wholesomeness. He was loved and cherished by his parents. His mother was such an intercessor, she literally used to weep into the pages of her Bible when she prayed and read Scripture. A home such as this today is a statistical rarity. Jon's testimony had been, "If you follow the Lord, He will bless you as He has me. You don't need to be a rebel." Jon could trace the moment of his salvation to the young age of three-and-a-half, when he consciously gave his life to Christ during an evangelistic rally as his parents held him in their arms. Jon remembers that moment as clearly as if it had been yesterday.

Yet, in the lives of even the best of Christians there are hard times, times of testing and times of drought. There are times that fire will consume some part of our lives to reveal what lies hidden. It is never easy. There are unexpected tragedies that come along and sift our souls in ways we never thought possible. And that is what happened to Jon. For one day, in one moment, the beautiful wife of his youth, Terry, was taken from him. It happened on a country road in Oregon, the winter of 1982, as Jon and Terry were driving down Highway 42 to Mount Bachelor. In an instant, his car slid on a sheet of ice, spun around, and slammed into a tree.

As he was crawling along the road looking for help he knew in his heart that Terry was dead. In the ambulance, the Holy Spirit spoke the words from Jeremiah 29:11 to him as it sped toward the town of Medford. The verse hung soberly in Jon's mind: *I know the thoughts that I think toward you. They are of peace and goodness and not of evil to bring you to a certain end.* Jon questioned why God had taken Terry, but never with bitterness, anger, or doubt. He was on an emotional roller-coaster. Yet beneath it he felt a peace that passes all understanding. God had assured him: *Jon, I have promised and given you a peace that passes all understanding. So do not seek a peace that comes from understanding. It does not work that way.*

Three years later, God gave Jon a beautiful wife named Tammy who has borne him two more children. She is lithe and young and loves him to pieces. Jon has learned that what Satan means for evil, God will turn for good through mercy and grace.

In 2002, I asked Jon to join me at Calvary Chapel, Costa Mesa. After serving with me for three years, Jon was called to a new ministry. He is leading a Pastor-in-Training School in Mexico for young men from the United States who are called to be pastors. When school is not in session, Jon is also teaching at churches, retreats and conferences around the country. His sons, Peter-John and Ben Courson, are both teaching and highly involved in ministry.

And that is the message of Jon's life and ministry. "As for me, I'm called to love. Our emphasis is on love." And many, in that expanding group of fellowships, have had vital encounters with the eternal love of Christ. There has been fire and rain in Applegate Valley and Jon has been blessed by being God's instrument in this.

Jon's life shows us that God is by no means limited to using converted rebels or people with heavy testimonies. Consider all of the Bible figures God used who came out of godly backgrounds. God can and will use any person who surrenders to Him. The only question is the willingness on the part of the individual.

Christ speaks of a party to which the aristocrats were invited. When they turned down the invitation, it became a beggars' banquet. They were the only ones needy enough to come. The rest were out there "making it" in the world. It is a rare thing for someone who "has it all" not to be tempted by worldly admiration and accolades, peer pressure and money, and the pleasures of life. It all comes too easily. That is why so few who do "have it all" are willing to sacrifice it all for the sake of the Kingdom of God. When they do, the results can be impressive as God uses them in His work.

R A U L   R I E S
FROM FURY TO FREEDOM

Born to a Spanish-American mother from New York, and a German-Mexican father from Mexico City, Raul Ries began life the hard way—accompanying his father from bar to bar in Mexico City. As a boy of nine, he witnessed more lewdness, drunken brawls, and sexual infidelity than any adult would in a lifetime. At home, Raul and his mother were often on the receiving end of his father's drunken fits of rage.

By the age of ten, already hardened by his father's fists and berating tongue, Raul defiantly stood up to his father's abuse, only to be knocked down again and again. The oldest of the three children at the time, Raul began to hate his father with an intensity that would shape his life for years to come.

During his tenth year, Raul's mother, weary of the constant violence and abuse in their home, took her children to Los Angeles to live with her parents. Raul's life became somewhat normal in America. His anger was soothed by baseball, a newspaper route, and serving as an altar boy in the Catholic Church. His peace, however, was short-lived. His mother told him one day that his father would be coming to their home for a visit. Raul knew better. One visit turned into others, and before long his father had moved back with the family in Los Angeles.

The drinking and abuse soon continued where it had left off in Mexico City, and so did Raul's anger and hatred. His one goal in life was to kill his father. As a result of his reaction to abuse, Raul also became skilled in hurting others, physically and verbally. By the time he was in high school, he feared no man. The biggest, toughest guys were his targets. His friends often had to drag him off a fallen victim to literally keep him from committing murder. Such was the case in 1966 at a party during his senior year of high school when Raul was arrested for beating a young man unconscious, kicking and pummeling the bloodied boy until Raul's friends managed to drag him off.

Raul soon found himself arrested and convicted of assault. With the Vietnam War beginning to escalate at the time, the courts gave him the choice of serving a prison sentence or enlisting in the military. Thinking that it would be a natural outlet for his anger and violence, he chose the military, enlisting immediately in the United States Marine Corps.

Although combat allowed him a release for his violent behavior, it also served to feed and propagate more of the same. He discovered that he truly enjoyed killing, which led to shameful acts of torture and murder that would cast a long shadow on the two Purple Hearts he won for being wounded in action.

While training a young man from Texas only a year younger than himself to lead a patrol, Raul began to get increasingly anxious, as his time in Vietnam was getting short. During a routine sweep of a Vietnamese village for booby traps, the novice tripped the detonator wire to an enemy grenade. At the spark of the grenade pin being pulled, Raul pushed the young man forward, yelling, "Grenade!" His actions were too late. The young man lost an arm and both legs. Raul himself took shrapnel down his entire backside.

After a couple of weeks recovery aboard the hospital ship *U.S.S. Sanctuary*, Raul was sent back to the bush. Having seen the grotesque wounds and vegetative state of many of the casualties in the *Sanctuary* hospital ward, he was apprehensive about going out on patrol. He felt that having been wounded twice, he should have been sent stateside. His anger and rage was turned from the Vietcong to his superiors. Aiming his weapon at his commanding officer, Raul threatened to kill him and a Navy psychiatrist. He was arrested and sent home to Oakland Naval Hospital's psychiatric ward for treatment.

Through a providential turn of events, Raul was honorably discharged from the Marine Corps. But his problems were only beginning. Not long after he returned home, he managed to get his backslidden Christian girlfriend pregnant, marry her, have a son, and begin to verbally and physically abuse his family. He also obsessively studied the martial art of Kung Fu San Soo until he earned a Master's black belt and opened his own studio. He could typically be found in the bars at night intentionally starting fights with the biggest, toughest guys he could find.

Despite swearing to himself that he would never become like his father, Raul began to physically and verbally abuse his wife, Sharon, and their children. After five tormenting years, his wife, who had re-committed her life to the Lord on their wedding day, packed her family's suitcases (they had two boys at the time) to leave while Raul was away on a weekend camping trip. Not expecting him home until late that Easter Sunday night, April 15, 1972, Sharon left all the luggage stacked neatly in the living room while she and her sons had gone to church. Raul arrived home early instead, and flew into a rage as he discovered that his wife and sons were leaving him. He decided then and there that he would kill her and his boys, and then either kill himself, or be killed in a shoot-out with the police.

Even though he had all the luxuries money could buy, different women every weekend, and fame and money from his martial arts studio, he was sick and tired of his life, feeling totally empty and drained. Nothing satisfied him any longer, but he could not admit that he was wrong.

He loaded his .22 rifle and paced the living room waiting for his family to get home. As he continued pacing, he turned on the TV and saw a program featuring testimony after testimony of young hippies who had surrendered their lives to Jesus Christ. These people seemed to radiate a genuine love that was somehow different than the phony hippie-type attempt at love that was popular at the time.

I was also on the program that night teaching about God's love: "God is perfect, and in His holiness, He can't have anything to do with us sinners. He loves us so much, however, that He Himself took the just penalty for all the sins in all of our lives. God wants you to know that in spite of what you may be or in spite of what you may have done—you may have messed up your life completely—God still loves you. He is reaching out to you and inviting you to come and to share that love with Him, no matter how deeply you may have gone into sin. Jesus offers forgiveness to us as a free gift. All we have to do is accept it, and surrender."

Raul's heart pounded. He put his rifle down, mesmerized by the words he was hearing. The longing for forgiveness overwhelmed him, but as a former Marine and Vietnam veteran he had thought that surrender was a sign of weakness. The spiritual struggle continued for minutes, but then Raul heard something in his heart tell him that this was his last opportunity. There would not be another time. He slipped off the chair and onto his knees in front of the TV screen, surrendering his life to Jesus Christ and becoming born again of the Holy Spirit.

He was so happy that he went looking for Sharon to tell her what had happened, but he could not find her. When he finally returned home, she was already there with the door securely locked. Raul knocked and pleaded, but Sharon would not open the door, crying and weeping out of fear that he was going to do harm to her and the children. After a long while of pleading, she finally opened the door, but only as far as the safety latch would allow.

Raul excitedly told her that he was born again. She slammed the door right in his face. After more pleading and persuading, she finally let him into the house. It took a year of closely watching his life to convince Sharon that he was serious about his commitment to Jesus Christ. She had seen so many husbands fake a relationship with God in order to get their wives back. Part of the proof was his commitment. As committed as he was to the martial arts, he became more committed to studying the Word of God. Sharon finally testified that God had truly worked His miracle of salvation in Raul as she saw that he was being transformed from the inside out.

No one told Raul to buy a Bible, or to read the Gospel of John. In fact, no one told him anything. Raul simply bought himself a huge family Bible, and began to read through the Scriptures in order. He also began driving ninety miles a day back and forth from West Covina to Calvary Chapel of Costa Mesa to hear the teaching of the Word of God in simplicity, excitement, and love.

He never introduced himself to me, or approached me in any way with his testimony or even desired to be in the ministry. He simply prayed and waited for the Lord to work. In the meantime, he began to study God's Word eight hours a day and listened to my through-the-Bible study tapes, coming out of his office only long enough to teach his Kung Fu classes. The Holy Spirit, not a Bible college or seminary, became his teacher.

During that time God also gave Raul a desire to go back to his old high school to teach and to preach. He was by no means a trained speaker. As a matter of fact, he could hardly read. His first visit back to the school ended with the principal having him thrown off campus. But not long after, the Lord again called him to go back. When he returned the second time, the principal gave him an opportunity to explain himself. After finally deciding that Raul was somehow different than he remembered, he allowed him on campus.

Over a period of six months, Raul simply read aloud to the students from the Bible during lunch period, and for six months all that happened was that he got pelted with food, napkins, and milk cartons. The experience was very frustrating for him.

Then one day something radically different happened, and Raul knew it was the work of God. The students were a little quieter than normal. After he read from the Bible he invited anyone who wanted to accept Jesus Christ as his or her personal Lord and Savior to come forward. He had never done that before, and he was amazed when four hundred students came forward wanting to receive Jesus Christ into their lives. Some of those same students have families of their own today and still fellowship with Raul at his church. That special day on his old high school campus, Raul recognized without a doubt, God's calling on his life.

With the calling, however, came the struggles. His family and friends no longer wanted him around. Raul became like the Black

Plague to them. It stung at first, but as he began to read the Word of God, he began to understand that the message of the cross of Christ will seem like foolishness to those who do not believe.

And yet, Raul was to receive another form of rejection which somehow hurt even more and made even less sense at the time. This time it came from the local churches in the San Gabriel Valley. He had approached virtually all of them to offer his help in working with their youth groups or young adults, only to be sent away with a cold, "No, thank you." In some instances he did not even receive that much. It seemed as though they felt threatened or intimidated by his enthusiasm. Consequently, he drove around the neighborhood and packed his van with young people from the streets, taking them to our tent meetings in Costa Mesa twice a week.

The rejection served a purpose in God's plan. It forced Raul to seek and find comfort in the Word of God alone. He had stumbled onto a biblical truth Charles Spurgeon expressed in this way, "The man who believes in God, and believes in Christ, and believes in the Holy Ghost, will stay himself upon the Lord alone." God Himself sustained Raul through those rejections, and would strengthen him through many more trials in the future.

Those first few years in the Lord were exciting for Raul as God spoon-fed him every day from His Word. The more he learned of God, the more he wanted to know. Even his reading and comprehension improved.

At some point during those first two years, Raul began a Bible study in his home with seven people listening to teaching tapes and discussing them afterward. None of them really expected to have a church or ministry. All they wanted to do was just love Jesus. They would gather together on Friday nights at a friend's house and pray all night long. In the morning, they would have breakfast and then continue throughout the day in fellowship with each other in the Lord. Week after week, month after month, and year after year, their ministry continued in prayer, waiting upon God to speak to them.

When they grew to fifty people, they finally moved their Bible study to Raul's Kung Fu studio, where they continued to go through the Bible with my tapes, because Raul still did not know how to teach. He did not feel that he *could* teach. God honored what they were doing—just sitting there and learning about Him.

For the first five years of ministry Raul's tiny congregation grew slowly. In retrospect, he realized that God was showing His faithfulness in providing all of his needs, and demonstrating that He was in control of His church.

During those five years Raul was tested severely, losing his Kung Fu business, not through neglect or mismanagement. He was so adamant about sharing the Gospel of Jesus Christ that most of his students eventually quit. He soon found himself having to work a part-time second job, and then full-time, as his business folded completely. God taught him many lessons about faith and dependence upon Him for all his needs.

Without a car, Raul would hitchhike to and from the ministry everyday. He decided to take advantage of his situation by using it as an opportunity to share Jesus Christ with many, many people he normally would not have met had he been driving his own car.

When Raul eventually attempted to teach on his own without the help of tapes, he taught the book of Ephesians with wonderful results. During the two years it took him to complete the book, his congregation expanded from fifty to five hundred people and outgrew the Kung Fu studio.

From the Kung Fu studio, Raul's church moved across the street to the Fox movie theater, carrying their own public address system in and out for every service. They set up the children's ministry and nursery at the Kung Fu studio, the barber shop, the insurance company, and another building that the landlord let them use. Cardboard boxes with blankets served as cribs for the babies.

Those were hard times of learning about the ministry for Raul, but again, God blessed, and the church grew from five hundred to about eight hundred people in a year-and-a-half. Raul added a second Sunday morning service to accommodate the crowds, but could not add a third service because the theater's matinee started at 1 p.m. and the church had to be out by noon.

One day, as he was driving home from a Bible study at his old high school, Raul spotted a vacant Safeway grocery store with a "For Sale" sign in the window. He took down the phone number, and called to tell the Realtor that his church was interested in purchasing the building. A real estate agent met him the following Monday and told him the price was $325,000.00 a lot of money in 1979. They would need a $5,000.00 down payment to begin escrow, but they only had $1,500 in the bank. Raul asked the Realtor if she would accept a $10 check to hold the property until Friday. Amazingly, she said yes, so he wrote her the check, and immediately called his elders to go to the mountains for three days to pray and seek an answer from the Lord.

On Thursday, he got a call from his secretary. She said that someone had dropped an envelope in the mail slot at his Kung Fu studio. Inside the envelope was a money order for $3,500. That amount plus the $1,500 in the bank equaled the $5,000 needed for escrow. God did the work, but He expected Raul to be obedient.

At the first Sunday morning service Raul had eight hundred people, all at once, in one place, with no pews, just folding chairs and lawn furniture. He was amazed and humbled by the work of God. The people were excited. The staff was excited. Raul thought, *God, You are too much. You allow me to teach Your Word and You bring all the people.*

By the second month in their new building, they were forced to go to two Sunday morning services because of the number of people being turned away. In six months they added a third Sunday morning service, and by year's end they were having four Sunday morning, two Sunday night, and two Wednesday night services.

Raul has learned over the years that the ministry demands tremendous sacrifices of himself, his family, his staff, and their families every week. But he clearly understands that that is the nature of the ministry—to serve, and to serve, and then to serve some more. When he begins to feel weary or overwhelmed, the Lord comforts him and reminds him that nothing done for Him is ever wasted or lost (Galatians 6:9-10; 1 Thessalonians 3:13). Raul also realizes how invaluable the sacrifices and trials are in building character in the individual and in the ministry (2 Corinthians 1:3-5, 4:16-18). His prayer is that Jesus Christ is always the center of his ministry.

The Lord's faithfulness has been manifested in Raul's life in many ways, but perhaps none more amazing than the work He has done in the lives of Raul's family members and friends. When he was first saved, Raul made a list of all of his friends from high school and began to pray fervently for their salvation, and one by one over the last twenty years each one has come to salvation through Jesus Christ, some of whom are even on his staff.

Raul's mother and two sisters are born again. His brother Xavier is the senior pastor of Calvary Chapel of Pasadena, and his brother-in-law, Gary Ruff, is the pastor of Calvary Chapel of the Foothills in La Canada. Even Raul's father, the man he hated so much and wanted so badly to kill, publicly gave his heart and life to Jesus Christ one night after Raul gave an invitation. What amazing things God is able to do through one man's obedience to Him.

Although he holds two masters degrees from Azusa Pacific University and a doctorate in theology from Fuller Theological Seminary, Raul has been gifted by God with the ability to transcend cultural, racial, ethnic, economic, educational, and intellectual barriers. God has used him to minister simply to the needs of people, *all* people, right where they are, regardless of their circumstances or station in life. On a typical Sunday, one can find the whole spectrum of our society gathered for worship. It is not uncommon to find gang members, college students, Vietnam veterans, professional athletes, and other respected professionals benefiting from Raul's gift of teaching. He has been gifted by God to effectively communicate and apply the eternal truth of the Word of God with great relevance for today's increasingly valueless society.

According to Tyndale Publishers' 1992 *Christian Almanac*, Calvary Chapel Golden Springs is ranked twenty-fifth among churches in size in the nation. As senior pastor, Raul teaches more than 12,000 people every week in Diamond Bar, California. He is also president of the Golden Springs School of Ministry. Raul's teaching is heard daily on the popular radio program *Somebody Loves You*.

His often humorous, always passionate, and ever practical teaching style, as well as his identification with *every man*, have earned him a popular following among real-life people with everyday struggles. He is definitely approachable and down-to-earth. His unique and excitable accent has also drawn a sizable

Hispanic audience. His life story, *From Fury to Freedom*, has been published by Harvest House Publishers, and the film version by the same title has been produced by Gospel Films. Raul's story is also available for kids in a three-part comic book.

Raul's wartime experiences are featured along with six other Vietnam veterans in a film for veterans and their families called *A Quiet Hope*. He has also produced (along with Mike MacIntosh) a two-hour video documentary on the history and philosophy of the Calvary Chapel movement entitled *A Venture in Faith*.

Raul simply loves to teach the Word of God with a passion that burns in his heart, taking the responsibility which God has given him as pastor/teacher seriously. He is not on an ego trip, but rather, desires that as many people as possible simply come to know and personally experience the same saving grace and knowledge of Jesus Christ which has set him free. His desire is to teach and preach the Word of God in any medium that presents itself, to anyone who will listen. To that end, his life has truly been a testimony to the saving grace and love of Jesus Christ.

J E F F   J O H N S O N
DRUG DEALER TO SHEPHERD

Jeff Johnson needed a lot of space. He settled himself deep in the jungle of Oahu, a Hawaiian island, surrounded by thick tropical foliage, absolutely alone. Jeff had been in Hawaii for several months in his pursuit of the "clear light." Now he was going to make the ultimate leap of his life. It was late summer 1968.

Jeff fasted for four days. He had brought a minimum of necessities and lived in a tent. His plan was to drop the biggest hit of LSD-25 he had ever taken, and as a drug pusher, Jeff had taken some enormous doses. But this time, he had an occult formula to follow. Jeff would become a modern shaman and follow an ancient path. Like Carlos Castaneda's accounts of his tutelage under an Indian sorcerer, Jeff was trying to meet with the primeval powers and forces to find a higher reality.

The film *Emerald Forest* portrays a white boy growing up deep in the interior of the jungles of Brazil. He was first kidnapped and then adopted by a tribe that had never contacted the modern outside world until bulldozers pushed deep into the Brazilian jungle. The youth learned to adopt their alternate way of thinking. He entered the shamanistic rites of the tribe at his initiation into manhood. On a powerful rare jungle plant, he experienced the ultimate psychedelic trip, and gained the shamanistic ability to turn into various animals. He could soar in the sky as a hawk. Or he could command the waters to rise, bringing on flood. The film is a seductive look into New Age beliefs concerning the psychic powers within, the inner self, oneness with nature, and mind-altering experiences. Jeff's rite in the jungle of Oahu, ten years before this film, certainly anticipated its teaching. He wanted to tap the hidden wisdom behind nature.

Before coming to the island of Oahu, Jeff had built up a considerable business pushing drugs in Southern California. He had managed to stay stoned on virtually any drug he wanted. But Jeff was also on a spiritual search. He had been pursuing the mystical teachings of Yogananda and the Self Realization Fellowship before leaving California.

Now Jeff was seeing a connection between Yogananda's teachings and the latest pronouncements of acid guru Timothy Leary, who often hung out in Hawaii. Instead of decades of yoga and astral travel and guidance through death planes, as the Tibetan Book of the Dead demanded of its adepts, Leary taught that it could now be done immediately with LSD. In fact Leary had translated this ancient Tibetan text in modern jargon and reset its rituals for LSD journeys. Acid was claimed to be the modern discovery providing instant access to the wisdom of the ancients.

Until that time, Jeff was living with fourteen others in a two bedroom communal house. It bordered the jungle within the interior of the island of Oahu. But there had been problems. Half the "freaks" were on LSD, and that was fine for Jeff. But the other half were on reds (downers) and that made for some bad communication. For instance, Jeff would be in the Lotus position, upside-down, trying to get his "third eye" to open. Then someone on reds would crash through the door with all the sensitivity of a bull in a china shop and ask, "Hey, man, what are you doing?"

Jeff would respond in irritation, "What do you mean, what am I doing? I'm getting in tune with God. You guys ought to clean up your act. You're taking all these downers and they're going to kill you. You ought to get where I am—in the high plane."

There were other rough edges to paradise. With everybody high and doing his own thing, nobody kept house. The dishes were stacked up to the ceiling. They were covered with mold and had started to smell. And fixing food was a major effort. Another thin edge to the dream was that most of the residents had to write home for money. They needed the straight world to keep them afloat.

So Jeff headed for isolation in the jungle. The acid that Jeff dropped there was tainted with strychnine, a rat poison. Dealers often cut LSD-25 with other chemicals (including strychnine) in smaller quantities. It was a popular diluting agent since it could act like speed. But in the quantities that Jeff took, it could be lethal. Countercultural chemistry had certainly gone beyond ethics. You did not always know what you were buying.

For two days, Jeff battled for his life. He retched and vomited almost nonstop while staggering and holding onto plants and trees. At night he swayed back and forth in the center of the tent. He entered a topsy-turvy realm of jungle fantasy. He had walked through the door of an alien universe. He began to believe he could hear ants and see and hear the bark of trees talking. Sounds came ripping through the jungle's interior that he never dreamed existed. After two days the strychnine effects wore off. At that point the LSD seemed to throttle his mind with full force.

On the third day a giant horsefly came into the tent and landed on Jeff's wrist. Jeff tried to hook his will to the fly with meditative force. He told the fly to flip over, and it did. Then he had it zooming patterns in the air. Jeff seemed to be able to get the fly to do anything. After several hours he let it go, mentally, and it flew out of the tent. As Jeff remembers, "The lord of the flies, Beelzebub, gave me a small sample of power."

It had been raining for two days. The sky had cleared and the air tingled with freshness. Jeff went outside and fell asleep on the jungle floor. He had been completely naked for some time. To Jeff's horror, he woke up in the early dawn with thousands of spiders and bugs all over him.

I will let him narrate this moment in his own words:

"I started to go out of my mind. I didn't know where I was. I started to panic. Fear took hold of me and I started to run through the jungle naked. Spider webs and all kinds of brush and tree branches swept by me as I ran out of control. I was scratched and bleeding. It was a terrible nightmare. I was lost in the jungle and had no idea how to get out. I had no clothes and I was totally disoriented. I began crying convulsively, knowing that I had lost my mind. Little did I know that God had His hand on me, protecting me through this deadly episode."

"All of a sudden I fell down over a cliff and rolled onto a main dirt road that led out of the jungle. I got on that road and ended up on the edge of a cliff that overlooked the north shore of Oahu. As I stood over the cliffs of Sunset Beach and Wihamea Bay, I felt Satan's presence. I began to chant the Sanskrit sound of "ohm"— the supposed primeval sound of the universe. My voice was getting louder and louder. As I had controlled the horsefly, I now wanted to control wider areas of nature in a godlike manner. This time I focused on the waves. Perhaps my senses were deceiving me, but I began to see it happen.

"My thoughts, as I chanted, were to bring the waves up from the sea to devour everybody who was down there. The waves were coming and I could see the swells getting bigger. Soon the massive waves ended up devouring everybody surfing in the ocean that day. And a number of homes below were wiped out. I felt I had access to infinite power and had finally tapped into the source, the hidden power behind nature. Yet I had not even seen the "clear light"—that was an indication to me of how great that "clear light" was. It was the cosmic carrot on the end of the stick."

The trip ended, and Jeff wandered back home down the old dirt road bordering the jungle. Since then, many of those who were members of Jeff's Hawaiian Timothy Leary LSD group, who claimed to see the "clear light," have died. Jeff now realizes that the pursuit of the "clear light" is one of Satan's secrets. But it amounts to little more than a doorway to possession. Jeff concludes,

"After my dream life of searching for God in Hawaii fell through, and I thought I was losing my mind, I tried to leave as soon as possible. The honey sweet drink of finding bliss in nature turned bitter. I finally sold my surfboard to help get my ticket home— aided by financial help from my parents. I felt like the eunuch who went to Jerusalem to find God, but left empty-handed. I was burned out by drugs and was homesick."

Once he was back home on the mainland, Jeff took another radical turn. He decided to abandon the search for God. He decided to try the straight world. "I will do what everybody says is the source of happiness." His new ambition was the American dream: a split-level home, wife, kids, a van, and even a dog—all made to order. That was the answer he now needed to fill the void inside of himself. And Jeff made it all happen. He even got a regular job for a while. "Here I was in my white picket-fenced home with a little dog, a good job, a child, and a wife." But the result was anguish as great as he had felt in Hawaii.

With all of his options burning out, Jeff was entering despair. An old friend came by and gave him a big black ball of Indian hashish laced with opium. Jeff felt the pull to turn back to drugs, and it began to fray the edges of his marriage. He knew there was a time fuse on his life. Something had to happen. While Jeff was smoking his hashish pipe one evening, he looked up at Karyn, his wife. She looked back at him and said, "Is this all that life is about? This is a bummer." Divorce looked inevitable. The American dream was crumbling and the returning drug world was no better.

Then one night another old friend, a big drug supplier, walked through his door—not with drugs but with a Bible in his hand. With intense conviction he told Jeff how Christ had entered his life and how he had given up the deadly world of drugs. Jeff was stunned. This was not some naive churchgoer with whom he could not identify, but one of his own kind, a heavyweight. His sincerity was undeniable. He even looked different. Jeff could feel powerful love coming from him. Finally, to placate his old friend, Jeff agreed to go with him to that evening's church service.

That night Jeff Johnson, former West Coast drug dealer and user, lawbreaker, and rebel, whose occult experiments had brought him to the brink of oblivion, walked forward to accept Jesus Christ as his Lord and Savior. He knew he was hearing the Truth. He had tried everything else, but it had all been seductive falsehood, sideshow games that had been rigged. The words of Christ had the ring of eternal truth.

Jeff changed dramatically and immediately. The Bible, which Jeff could never quite understand, now started to make incredible sense that very night. From then on he poured over its pages, absorbing its great truths. Why had he not seen it all before? Because his mind was previously darkened. God had to open Jeff's eyes.

Jeff's changes in life and character were so intense that within six months, his wife finally left. He was no longer the same man. In fact, she even preferred his drug excesses over his newfound passion. As far as she was concerned, he was worse as a zealot for Christ than as a doper. His zeal for the Lord was boundless. Indeed, perhaps it was a little too raw-edged, too insensitive to the acceptable boundaries of others and needed to be tempered.

Within two weeks of Jeff's conversion, he started to come to Calvary Chapel Costa Mesa regularly. He came for four years and sat under my teaching, after which he felt equipped to start his own church. We had been through the Bible twice by then. Jeff was an avid learner and passionate apologist for the faith.

When Jeff's wife had first separated from him, he joined up with six other fellows and started a Christian commune in Downey, a suburb of Los Angeles. It was called the Philadelphia House, and sixty to eighty high school students were coming there each night to hear Jeff teach. But the local neighbors were suspicious, connecting it to a Manson-type cult. The police would come almost nightly with helicopters and car raids, but all they ever found were serious disciples avidly sharing their faith.

At this time Karyn was off with another man and back into drugs and partying, though she confessed later that she felt absolutely empty inside. Jeff was praying for her, but he was not about to return to that lifestyle. He had found reality, finally. Meanwhile, Karyn had even found a counselor, a "professional," who agreed with her that Jeff was brainwashed, fanatical, and should be divorced. But despite the bad advice, Karyn did come back. They spent months working very hard on reconciliation, going to marriage counseling, and doing a lot of praying and communicating together.

After those four years of attending Calvary Chapel Costa Mesa, Jeff and Karyn's marriage was healthy and grounded. The Lord had guided them through their initial problems and growing pains. But the tough times were not completely over yet. The pastorate would extract unanticipated demands.

Jeff began to feel that he had a mission in his hometown. He felt called to be a pastor. He also knew that Downey needed a church similar to Calvary Chapel. So for a year, Jeff became the part-time, unofficial youth pastor at a church in Downey. But soon Jeff became distressed over all of the politics, inefficiency, back-stabbing, and manipulation that he saw there. The church was not reaching the huge needs of Downey, which he termed "a spiritual desert." Meanwhile Jeff's weeknight Bible study was drawing more people than the pastor's, and envy resulted. The pastor closed down Jeff's study for a while until requests of the parishioners brought it back. Time and again he would be grieved no end as he saw God's work actually hampered from within that church—the very vessel that should be bringing the truth to the world. It was a tragic irony.

One evening God indicated to Jeff that he was to leave the church and begin a Calvary Chapel. He was to start from scratch.

So, in May of 1973, he began what was to become Calvary Chapel of Downey in the unlikely sight of Furman Park. It was simple and natural. His first turnout was ten people. There was not the slightest indication of the staggering size that this fellowship would one day become. Jeff felt that Downey was his area, given to him by God. But there were some things Jeff still had to learn before the real harvest came.

When the rainy season arrived, Jeff was given a feeling by the Spirit of where to drive to look for his new building—Downey Avenue and Fourth Street. And there it was: an old store. It could hold a hundred per service. Jeff says of this era in his ministry: "This is the place where God started to show me what it was to be a pastor and how to have a shepherd's heart. What it was to have a commitment to people, to love them, to teach them, and to learn to trust the Lord to do his work. This was my spiritual wilderness where God really dealt with me and only then did we gradually start to grow. By the end of those two-and-a-half years, we were up to two hundred people."

Then the harvest for Downey began. Jeff and the Downey Calvary Chapel started to move to different facilities as the fellowship grew. One day, in March of 1977, his church accountant told Jeff prophetically, "You will need to find a building that will seat fifteen hundred people." At the time, this comment seemed preposterous.

But sure enough, as Jeff was driving down the freeway one day, his eye was drawn to the Downey Civic Center, a multimillion dollar theater that held 750. He felt that he should at least go through the motions of trying to get it for Sunday mornings. When he expected the manager to laugh in his face in response to using it, he heard instead a cheerful "That will be no problem." But when Jeff walked out on the stage and saw the large auditorium his response was, "Oh, no. I can't do this Lord." God assured Jeff that it would be done through Him and that no man would get the glory, but God alone.

Soon after the accountant's prophetic remark, Jeff started services in the Downey Civic Center. Six months later, the crowds were so great that Jeff was forced to hold two services on Sunday mornings. And that equaled 1,500 people, as the prophecy had foretold.

But Jeff was facing a hidden foe that has been a classical stumbling block to pastors for centuries. It may be the greatest bane, the most difficult obstacle that any pastor faces. It has also undone many a ministry. I am referring to the needs of one's own family that conflict with what seem the infinite needs of one's church. Although Jeff's ministry was thriving, it was fast becoming a desert experience to those whom he loved the most, his family.

Jeff has told audiences what was at stake. He says:

"During all this growth and busy time with the church, I had gotten into an affair. Not with a woman, but with the church. My family was suffering, especially my wife. She was going through some real changes. And my being gone so much did not help matters. She started to withdraw after a hard experience in a women's group. She was crying a lot and I thought that she just needed more Bible and fellowship (the convenient 'easy answer'). But in reality she was on the verge of a nervous breakdown. We found out years later that Karyn had a fear of crowds. I was at my wit's end.

"Finally, my wife and I went to an old friend for marriage counseling. That is when God hit me with Acts 1:8, that I was not taking care of 'Jerusalem' first. My home was my ministry, my church was my calling. I preached it, told young couples about it, but I was failing to do this myself. I had to repent and change my actions to love my wife as Christ loved the Church. Ever since then, our marriage has been growing and getting stronger. Eventually, my wife beat the fear of crowds with God's help."

Jeff also faced problems with the Civic Center. Special events would override the church's use of the auditorium. The inconvenience and continual growth seemed to put Jeff into an impossible situation. How do you get any bigger than the local civic center? What around was any bigger?

Once Jeff faced his family problems, with God's help, God proved once again that He is able to solve impossible situations. Jeff was now ready for the next thing God had in store for his ministry.

If you have ever seen the largest of the Target stores, they are almost the size of an indoor mall. In California we had a chain of stores that were perhaps even bigger than Target called "White Front." The one in Downey, which was no longer being used, was stupendous. It had twelve acres just for parking cars.

In May 1978, only five years after Jeff had started his small fellowship in Furman Park, Calvary Chapel of Downey moved into the colossal facility—150,000 square feet under a single roof. That equals three football fields!

On February 8, 1980, a year-and-a-half after they moved into the massive new facility, the *Los Angeles Times* did a feature article on this church, headlined "Downey's Largest." They mentioned the 1,500-seat sanctuary that was being built, and the fact that a total of 5,000 were showing up Sunday mornings during the three overflow services. Some of the building space was being set aside for a school.

The *Times* article began with the words, "The growth of Calvary Chapel, located in an old White Front store at Woodruff and Imperial highways in Downey, can only be considered phenomenal." A picture of Jeff in front of the facility was featured. In the month before the article was written, the attendance of the church, according to the staff writer, had increased by five hundred people. In that single month, the church gained twice the number of members that Jeff had in his first two years of ministry.

Today the church is still growing. In November of 1990, they completed a new sanctuary that seats nearly 4,000 people. But Jeff disavows that it is from any charisma on his part—he is an onlooker. It is God who is allowing this to happen. Jeff feels that he is called to be faithful and not look to himself. The focus is on God and trying to meet people's needs.

When Jeff speaks, it is from a grounding in both worldly experience and heavenly wisdom. He is warm and transparently honest. The church members know that one who talks about his own battles with lust or unbelief is anything but a spiritual phony.

Jeff's eyes are on the contemporary battles of our society. For instance, he erred in junior high school and he knows exactly what young people are going through when they become parents outside of marriage. Since both Jeff and Karyn have been an unwed father and mother themselves, they have a burden for unwed mothers.

Because of this experience, they began a ministry called the House of Ruth to meet the needs of a crisis pregnancy. Jeff also addresses this contemporary problem on the air. He counsels people who face tough choices. Should a pregnant high school girl, who has become a Christian, try to marry the teenaged father, bring up her baby alone, or give it to a responsible couple for adoption? And if she is not a Christian, how do you get her to see that abortion is murder and something that she will have to live with the rest of her life? These are some of the issues that Jeff's ministry has had to address.

And what about drugs? He deals with this problem during Sunday services, and on the radio and has a ministry that helps substance abusers dry out. The ministry also counsels people with a variety of critical problems, including those in the middle of domestic disputes, those on the brink of suicide, and those who have OD'd on drugs.

Calvary Chapel of Downey has spawned a number of support ministries including a theater company, concerts, movies, a nationwide daily radio ministry called "Sound Doctrine," various missions outreaches, meal services, a shelter, a prison ministry, family counseling, and evangelistic crusades, to name only a few. Jeff has been called to speak all over the world. He has given pastors' conferences in Egypt and other parts of Africa, where he has also spoken at Gospel crusades.

Jeff acts on his strong conviction that the Church is the world's primary agent holding out the bright light of God's revelation, truth, and grace. His ministry stresses the importance of living out the Gospel of Jesus Christ in faith and action, but that is only possible through the enabling power of the Holy Spirit.

To put Jeff's story in perspective, picture once again that nude youth running through the jungles of Oahu on LSD and rat poison in the hands of occult powers. Picture a former drug pusher who showed such signs of utter incorrigibility that everyone gave up on him from the third grade onward. He had to forge records just to graduate from high school. Picture a man so committed to sin, that organized crime was at his door.

Now picture this same man with the colossal ministry outreach of an overflowing church in Downey. Can this magnitude of change in a person's character and life be anything short of an act of God? Could Karl Marx or Sigmund Freud change such a life from the inside out? Hardly. For, you see, though Marx could give someone a cause, and though Freud might make that cause an understanding of one's self, neither could fill the inner void of a soul with love. Love is the great miracle, the missing ingredient in all these causes. Such love is a supernatural gift of divine grace from a sovereign God.

Ask Jeff Johnson where this love came from, and you'll receive an answer from the blind man who now sees. And from Jeff's own mouth you hear the words, "Jesus Christ, the Savior of the world, entered me one day, forgave my untold sins, and then changed me forever." Only God's Messiah can do that.

Sharing his testimony has inspired Jeff to write his autobiography entitled, *The Seeker*, illuminating Jeff's life as the Senior Pastor at Calvary Chapel of Downey. Also included is his call to ministry, his family's involvement, and the growth of Calvary Chapel of Downey. *The Seeker*, available from Calvary Distribution and chapel stores, is now in its second edition which includes a special audio CD at the back of the publication.

CHAPTER
9

S K I P   H E I T Z I G

A Quest For Psychic Powers

In 1981 there was no Calvary Chapel in the state of New Mexico. Today the massive Calvary Chapel of Albuquerque has become the largest church in the state. It started out as a Bible study, then became a church, and started moving from facility to facility as it grew. Finally the fellowship bought "The Sports Center," a huge complex with an indoor soccer field, racquetball courts, and offices. They installed 1,800 seats on the soccer field after pulling up the Astroturf and replacing it with carpet. It was hoped that this new facility was now big enough to allow them to hold only one Sunday morning service. But from the moment the renovated complex opened, the crowds spilled over into two Sunday morning services. Attendance at Calvary Chapel of Albuquerque jumped to 4,000 adults on the first day in this new facility!

The instrument God used in this is Skip Heitzig, a handsome six-foot-four fellow. All Skip knew, from the time he became a Christian in the early '70s, and faithfully attended and worked with Calvary Chapel, was that he was supposed to leave California one day and plant a church. Later on he knew it was to be somewhere in the Southwest. In 1981 Skip and his wife moved to Albuquerque and started a Bible study. There was a period of intense trial, but from then on it grew.

If you look at Skip today, he looks as straight as they come. You would never guess his past. That alone testifies to what the Holy Spirit can do in a believer's life. Skip grew up in the high desert country of Southern California, reaching his mid-teens when the '60s turned into the '70s. He was going along a peculiar and dangerous road when the Lord stood at an intersection to hail him down.

PLAYING WITH PSYCHIC POWERS

In 1971 Skip and Gino, a close friend, were both sixteen and in high school. They had broken away from the rest of their high school tour group, and were camping out in a hotel room in Mazatlan, a subtropical region along Mexico's Pacific coast. From there they hoped to contact the spirit world.

Gino had a reputation for reading people's fortunes with tarot cards. But their goal was to get the spirits to take them over and write messages through them by "automatic writing." They both sat in their hotel room for a couple of nights waiting to make contact.

Skip was in a trance. His hand held a pen poised over a piece of paper. He was sending out messages, asking the spirits to take control of his arm and write messages about his past lives. Was he a former Atlantean high priest or Indian mystic?

Mazatlan's damp night ocean air started howling through the windows. The curtains flapped. An electric presence seemed to fill the air. Skip's arm started moving out of his control. The pen scribbled meaninglessly for a while. Then words started to form: "You were in the Franco-Prussian war where you were killed." Skip and Gino were alarmed, then frightened. What had they summoned? Then the spirit gave him a message: "Skip, you are going to die on your way home from Mazatlan." Now they were scared to death. After a few hours, well past midnight, they lay in their beds trying to go to sleep, occasionally discussing what it meant. Would they really be killed on the train journey back to California?

In the early hours of the morning a light caught Skip's attention. A shining thing was bouncing up and down the wall. It seemed to be part of the message. He cried out to Gino and they discovered that moonlight was reflecting off a dagger that laid by Skip's bedside. They did not know how the dagger got there. Skip suddenly understood: "We're going to get knifed to death on the train!" For a while, they refused to go back home. Then, when they finally agreed to return with the group, nothing happened.

With the idea of reincarnation Skip felt a new freedom. If he had endless lifetimes before him to experience things, he could throw each one away like a cigarette. There would always be another life, why not try new thrills? He and his rock band started to burn entire lids of Acapulco gold marijuana in a sealed-off practice room. One night he and a friend took off on a new adventure. Hours later they were in a police station, busted for grand larceny. His father grounded him for a month, but Skip smiled inwardly. He had rarely been happier than when he was committing the crime. He figured that God wanted him happy, and that crime made him happy, so God approved it. He also kept pursuing his quest for psychic powers. In trances he would find items that he had lost for years. He would be "guided" to where they were. A whole new realm appeared to be opening before him.

Then Skip started studying about astral projection. He learned to lie in a trance, his body paralyzed, a loud buzzing sound in his ear. Suddenly he would seem to leave his body behind. At one point Skip and Gino decided to meet as spirits in the lobby of the Mazatlan Hotel. They compared notes, after sensing each other there. They discovered they had seen similar faces in the bar.

Skip's next experiment was geared to impress a girl who was "Miss Victorville" and a model, now a fellow student in his high school photography class. "I can project into your bedroom," he challenged. She laughed in his face. So he vowed to show her.

Skip lay back in his bedroom, went into a trance, and seemed to leave his body as he willed himself into her bedroom. He saw her reading in bed, examined her room, the red curtains, and then tried to leave a mental message that he was there.

Back in class he told her the entire layout of her room, the moment he had appeared, and that he had seen her reading. She looked horrified. Then he said he had been hovering near the foot of her bed. She reported that at that exact time, she looked on the floor and saw a flat piece of paper suddenly crumple up into a ball on the floor. "That was me," Skip replied with a knowing smile. "I knew something made you aware that I was there in spirit." She covered her mouth then said, "You're weird. Get out of here."

The bass player in the band tried astral projecting on LSD and almost got killed by running into oncoming traffic. He thought he was a spirit while still in his body. Some years later, he was busted for selling half-a-million dollars worth of synthetic heroin.

Meanwhile Skip's hatred for his father, an aloof and demanding perfectionist who had shown him little affection from as far back as he could remember, was becoming pathological. Skip was beginning to plot his father's death. He also enjoyed giving his mother sadistic little messages like, "Mom, I hate Dad and I'm going to kill him."

His father fully expected Skip to be class valedictorian, like his two oldest brothers. Like them, Skip was ordered to follow a tight academic regimen while shooting nine holes of golf daily and learning public speaking, all in a well-planned pursuit of a successful career. But no effort of Skip's was ever enough to earn his father's approval, so he stopped trying. Instead Skip viewed this sterile plan with scorn, choosing instead to shock his parents. Nor was Skip the only son to rebel against this cold disciplinarian. He had a brother Bob, two years older, who was six-foot-eight and rode his Harley with the Hell's Angels. Apparently he was brilliant, but thought of his father with contempt. One time the father slapped Bob. In turn Bob knocked him through a door and sent him flying down the hallway. Bob, like Skip, left home while still in his teens. When he was twenty-four, he was killed in a motorcycle crash.

THE ETERNAL DIVIDE

By the time Skip was eighteen and on the verge of attending San Jose State in 1973, which he really didn't want to do, he knew his life was going nowhere. Skip had tried everything—all the thrills of Southern California, from drugs to surfing to rock-and-roll—and it left him bored and frustrated. None of these things gave him their promised happiness. Skip could find no clear hold on what he should do. And the psychic channels were like a minefield. For every item of value he came up with, he had to sort through heaps of garbage that came along with it.

Skip was spending the summer in the house of one of his two older successful brothers who lived in San Jose, Northern California. It was a quick drive from San Francisco and its East Bay counterparts of Berkeley and Oakland. Unlike the high desert, the summers here were gloriously cool, the air full of evergreen smells. Within an hour Skip could ride his motorcycle to the Stanford campus, or be on the other side of the bay where the motley crew along Telegraph Avenue flowed onto the radical campus of UC Berkeley.

One day Skip sat alone watching TV. The one thing Skip did learn to prize from his father was the art of good communication. He was mesmerized by the face of a man on TV addressing a packed stadium. His blue eyes pierced through the screen. His voice echoed soul-searching questions, then paused with dignity. The words electrified Skip with things he had never heard or considered before.

It was Billy Graham. Skip felt as if the voice were cutting into him, peeling away his detached critical edge. The meaning of the words now began to convict him. For the first time in his life, Skip Heitzig was hearing the Gospel of Jesus Christ through the mouth of probably the greatest evangelist of our era. Skip sensed he had a choice that he did not really want to face. He considered turning the TV off before the clincher came, some question about commitment. But he waited and suddenly realized that he was glad to be sitting home alone and not out there in the open stadium where hundreds were coming forward. He knew that if he were there, he would probably be walking up the aisle himself. But he was safe in his room, no one could see him.

Then the piercing eyes looked into the camera at the TV audience. "Wherever you are, whether you are in a bar, or a hotel room"—Skip's stomach knotted—"you too can turn your life over to Jesus Christ, right there where you are. You can kneel down and pray the sinner's prayer." Graham echoed the words of the sinner's prayer. And Skip, within the inner chambers of his soul, did the same. He was now doing what he said he would not do. Skip thought to himself: *Lord, You're getting a rotten deal. I'm giving You all this crudeness and meaninglessness in me. And You're giving me eternal life in return and blessing me. I would have to be an idiot to turn this down.* He was kneeling and praying. In a mere moment, what seemed like a million-pound weight was removed from him.

Within a matter of days Skip Heitzig was on his motorcycle making the nine-hour ride from the Bay Area back to Southern California. He quit the new job he had just gotten and withdrew from college. He felt joy for the first time in his life, as he sang the whole way home.

Once in the high desert of Victorville he met one of his old friends who was at the Macedonia House, one of the Calvary Chapel communes that my brother Paul Smith directed with Steve Mays. Skip's friend was now a Christian. He immediately asked Skip, "Have you been born again?" Suddenly there was a word that described what had happened to him. And there was even a Scripture for it, John 3:3-8. His soul had been washed and made new. Skip had changed and been given a new nature.

From then on Skip worked with Macedonia House and got grounded in the faith. He found out that a number of his old friends had been converted and had been praying for him. On Sundays Skip would come down from the high desert to Calvary Chapel Costa Mesa to hear me teach. My brother soon got Skip into a situation where he was forced to teach a Bible study. And that was when Skip discovered he had a gift.

Skip kept plugging into various Calvary Chapels after he moved from the Macedonia House to San Bernardino where he worked on a two-year degree in radiology. I had told him that for ministers starting a church, it was not a bad idea to have an occupation that you can take with you anywhere in order to underwrite your ministry. Skip got his degree in 1975. Then he moved near Calvary Chapel Costa Mesa and taught Bible studies while he continued waiting for God to direct his path in the church-planting ministry.

During these years of growth, Skip made peace with his father. It happened after his brother was killed in the motorcycle accident mentioned earlier. Skip saw his father at the funeral and knew that the Lord would have him show his father the love of Christ. He grabbed his father and said a prayer out loud: "Lord, thank You for my dad. I love him. He's been a gift to me. He's been a great dad." It stunned Skip's father as the two stood there teary-eyed. If anything could signal a change in Skip's life to his father, it was this new love and meekness. Since that time the two have grown closer. And now these two fellows who never hugged, hug every time they see each other.

Skip relates that only two weeks before his brother's death, he felt God's clear direction late one night after a Bible study. He was to go by his brother's house nearby and witness to him. His brother had always violently rejected Skip's Christianity. Skip told this bitter Hell's Angel, "You just don't know when you are going to die. Life could end anytime." And it did. Sadly his brother had only laughed.

GOD PROVIDES A MATE AND A MINISTRY

By 1978, Skip had been a Christian for five years. He was zealous and eager, teaching and sharing anytime he could, while keeping his eye on the horizon to see where he might plant a church. He met Lenya that year at one of the church functions. When she was in college, her dad, an agnostic medical doctor, had written a book on positive thinking entitled, "How to Make Your Dreams Come True". He had decided that Jesus might be a good example. But when he read the Bible, something happened: He became converted. Lenya soon followed her father's footsteps. Like him, she began involving herself in Calvary Chapel's ministries to learn and be built up as a disciple after having dropped out of college. Suddenly she was stopped in her tracks by this tall, handsome fellow. Lenya, a bright, good-looking girl, immediately attracted Skip's attention as well, and they dated for six months.

Then Skip backed out. He was afraid of commitment. He had seen precious little love in his own family, and he was afraid of the risks of emotional vulnerability. Besides, he told himself, he was a more mature Christian, and now a responsible leader, while Lenya was a recent convert. They just weren't on the same wavelength.

Soon after his brother died, Skip left Lenya in Orange County and headed to Israel to work on a kibbutz. In the meantime, Lenya joined Youth With A Mission and spent two years in Hawaii. She grew in her faith, but her longing to marry Skip and be a pastor's wife grew as well. To her, this was a high calling indeed. Such desires were against the tide of feminism as well as her career-oriented peers, who felt she should be "out there doing something." But Lenya knew where her heart was. Skip was her dream husband, friend, and companion.

Her father knew all about his daughter's yearning. Now if it wasn't going to happen, Dr. Farley wanted to end the uncertainty for Lenya's sake, so that she would be able to get on with her life. He did something rare for modern fathers these days.

Skip had decided that the Lord wanted him to start his church in New Mexico. Just when he was on the verge of moving in 1981, Dr. Farley called him. "Skip, I love my daughter enough to make this call and tell you what she would never tell you. Skip, she is in love with you. If you love her, too, I want you to tell her. You owe it to her to tell her how you feel. If you do not love her, then tell her you do not want anything to do with her. But let her know either way, so she can get on with her life." Skip was stunned. Like the old days, the father was looking after his daughter and almost arranging a marriage. Skip could only reply, "I didn't know she loved me."

Skip moved tentatively. He sent her a fishy, rambling letter with a picture of himself holding a surfboard. She wrote back a letter so vulnerable and self-revealing that a friend had to mail it for her. In it she came right out with her desire to marry Skip, to be a pastor's wife, and to move to a new area. Skip read it trembling. He felt his own heart being expressed by her words. He sent her a bouquet of flowers. His follow-up letter a week later said, "I love you."

Lenya returned in the spring of 1981 from Hawaii and Skip was there to meet her, holding a rose for her. They drove straight to the beach to pray. Then they talked nonstop for three days. Within two months, on June 13, 1981, they were married, and two weeks after that, they moved to Albuquerque.

All of these changes at once—a new marriage, a new job for Skip in radiology, a new ministry (a Bible study in their apartment), and a new town—put a lot of pressure on the couple. On top of everything else Skip was depressed by the weather. He was used to Southern California winters in the mid-seventies, full of sunny days and blue skies. Somehow, he had not considered the cold of the New Mexico high lands before making the move. In fact they were both under a lot of stress, causing them to cry almost every day for a while.

Skip had promised God a year in New Mexico, but he decided that six months was enough. When they took a Christmas vacation in California Skip said, "Lenya, I belong back here." But Lenya was apprehensive about leaving. Then God spoke to Skip's heart, *You owe me six months,* and Skip knew it was true.

Reluctantly he returned to New Mexico. Skip now says that those were the most incredible six months of his life.

Right before Valentine's Day of 1982, they started Sunday services in a movie theater. This was just after Raul Ries had come to town and held a crusade. Skip was sure the spacious movie theater would be empty, but 150 showed up. By June all 300 of the seats were filled on Sunday mornings. They moved to a renovated storefront with 400 seats, and within a few months, they had to remodel it to seat 550. By 1983 they had to switch to two services.

Next they moved to a shopping center with a facility that would seat 900. That was in 1984. They stayed there two years, again doubling to two services. When the landlord made conditions intolerable, because of his violently anti-Christian stance, the way opened for them to buy the Sports Center. Every obstacle was swept aside, and with each change of course Skip saw his fellowship grow into a bountiful harvest.

Today Skip and Lenya have deeply fulfilled lives with a happy family and a healthy church. Skip is on the radio daily in New Mexico and other regions. Gino, Skip's high school friend, is now a Christian and is pastoring a Calvary Chapel in Colorado. A number of churches have sprung up from the ministry of Calvary Chapel of Albuquerque, including Calvary Chapels in Tucson and Denver, and four other churches in New Mexico. Skip and Lenya's burden for the mission field has been fulfilled as well. Skip has gone to India to give pastors' conferences. They now have a school of ministry there, training people to go out into the mission field and start new churches.

Those demonic spirits that moved Skip's arm in the Mazatlan hotel room could only offer him death threats. But the sovereign

God who moved Skip's entire life has brought him a richness and depth of life, a hope and a joy, a quality of being, and a harvest of souls, that have surpassed Skip's wildest imaginings.

God also brought him a beautiful wife who loves her Lord and her husband. She has brought beauty to Skip's life and enriched it. She has helped make all the difference in the world to his ministry.

Skip listened to God at each turn, and let Him build his life into something that no personal strategy could have ever accomplished. In this tapestry of lives, we see a former psychic becoming a great vessel of the Lord. He who was once influenced by demonic spirits is now governed and indwelt by the Holy Spirit. These two states, as Skip will tell you, are a universe apart, as the fruit of Skip's life, before and after, clearly shows.

As Paul the apostle was relating his conversion experience to King Agrippa, he said that Jesus sent him to the Gentiles to turn them from darkness to light, from the power of Satan to God. This describes what happened to Skip. He testifies to others that there is no life so dark that the light of Jesus cannot shine in and cleanse and make new.

CHAPTER
10

" BIL " GALLATIN

VISION OF DESTRUCTION

Thriving Calvary Chapel fellowships, are by no means just a West Coast phenomenon anymore. The harvest that we have seen in the Western United States is now beginning to appear in the Midwest, the Southwest, and now the East Coast.

It has been particularly heartening to see those who live back East laying aside apprehension about a "non-traditional" church and opening their hearts to our fellowships. I think the stories of "Bil" Gallatin and Joe Focht beautifully illustrate a growing willingness to allow the fresh breeze of the Spirit blow in. Bil and Joe moved east with their mustard seed faith, prayed for God's grace, persevered, and God brought in the harvest. As always, they started with a Bible study and watched it grow into a church.

Not too long ago, I flew back from an East Coast pastors' conference in Upstate New York with around a hundred of our East Coast ministers in attendance. It was a thrilling experience to see what is happening in these fellowships. We even ordained a member of the philosophy faculty at West Point who has started a Calvary Chapel fellowship there. Pastors came in from Pennsylvania, New Jersey, Illinois, North Carolina, Georgia, South Carolina, Ohio, Tennessee, Virginia, and New York City, where we have a fellowship meeting in a dance studio with up to five hundred members. Greg Laurie, flew to New York a few years ago to help start the Manhattan fellowship.

If we examine the East Coast growth of Calvary Chapel, I would have to point to Bil Gallatin's Maranatha Fellowship near the city of Rochester, New York, as the foundational work. It had been a home base for many of the other Calvary Chapels, with Bil serving as a voice of encouragement to many starting fellowships.

Maranatha Fellowship exploded in a ten-year period. It met in a roller skating rink that had seated well over a thousand, and had three morning services on Sundays. Thirty years ago Bil Gallatin was on staff at Calvary Chapel Costa Mesa as a carpenter. Before that he was a construction worker, college dropout, and at one time a hippie.

When Bil was converted in early 1970, this 220-pound man with a thick beard and long hair came to our fellowship in denim overalls. He had recently sold his .357 magnum revolver. Bil was no one you wanted to mess around with.

Bil ended his brief attendance at Bowling Green State University, Ohio, in the late '50s, when he beat a person senseless on campus. With a warrant out for his arrest, he fled and joined the Marines. When Bil got out in 1960, he married Rosemary, but continued drinking and getting into fights. He worked various jobs in Ohio while his marriage continued to deteriorate. In 1968 Bil and Rosemary looked to California for sunshine, hope and new identities. It was there that Bil discovered psychedelics and the occult. After a number of bad experiences he was ready to meet Jesus Christ. At the time when Bil walked into my office in early 1970, the countercultural phenomenon had reached its peak.

A month or so before I first saw this wild-eyed man, Bil Gallatin had been on one of his last psychedelic trips. He had been sitting in a coastal cemetery overlooking the Pacific Ocean near Corona Del Mar, when he beheld a vision that he described to me as the end of the world. He saw the coastline being consumed in nuclear fire, and everything being destroyed. A terrible smog sat over Santa Catalina Island. Atomic bombs went off in series from there down to Los Angeles. America sank like the Titanic. The vision convinced

Bil that modern man did not have the answers to existence, that as a steward of the world, he was destroying all that he touched. A few weeks after this experience, Bil accepted Christ. But he wanted a Christian to talk to, so he ended up driving into our parking lot and walking right over to my office. Bil had a long way to go before he was fully healed, but he had taken a strong step of faith. He was sure that Christ was the Son of God, but there were deep rooted problems still in need of God's healing.

A CASE OF POSSESSION

Not too long before our conversation, Bil had gone through a rather ironic experience at a psychiatric holding tank. When he went there with his wife, he was sure they were going to commit her. But they kept him instead, strapping him down and wheeling him through huge metal doors. This was grim humor indeed. Rosemary was later told that Bil was a hopeless case and that she had better get used to the fact that he would probably not be coming out. His long months of bizarre behavior-evident telepathy, imaginary visitors for dinner, and long binges on mescaline and LSD—had taken their toll.

But the real problem was not mental, it was spiritual, even demonic. There were times that the violence Rosemary felt lurking beneath Bil's powerful presence seemed almost volcanic. He had a long history of fights, necessitating that she go down and get him out of jail time and again. In truth she had sensed something alien inside of Bil, but she had no idea what it was. Neither of them knew anything about the reality of demonic possession, though Bil had been afraid that something terrible was going on inside of him.

He remembered when it began. He was on a week-long drug binge in Baja, Mexico, in early 1968. He and a small group of friends on the beach explored the outer limits of freedom. It was then that he saw an image of Satan in the beach bonfire one night. It was hideously beautiful and captivating. Its message to Bil was, "Don't be afraid. There is nothing in the world to be afraid of."

Bil continued to use psychedelics. Some months later, following a three day high, he walked into his house, stood in the doorway of the kitchen, and stared Rosemary in the eyes. She was terrified. An overpowering force thrust down his spine, knocking Bil on his back. Something had entered him. He felt a new power inside of himself. Suddenly he could read Rosemary's mind. He had access to any of her thoughts and she could no longer keep secrets. As he got off the kitchen floor and stood up again in the doorway, his eyes and appearance seemed to change dramatically. From that time on, and for the next two years, Rosemary lived in fear.

Bil refers to his exorcism as a sovereign act of God. It took place in the kitchen of a nearby house they had moved into. No one else was there. Bil had been reading the Bible, and experiencing considerable adversity while doing so. It had been nearly two years since he had been possessed, yet he had still come to the realization that Jesus was the Son of God. At two in the afternoon, Bil was suddenly knocked flat on his back. As he lay on the kitchen floor, he convulsed and twisted helplessly.

The thought pressed in on his mind: *There is no hope for me. This is it. I'm finished.* Then he suddenly called upon the name of Jesus. He mouthed the words, "Jesus, help me!"

Bil's body suddenly became motionless as something seemed to expel out of him. He lay absolutely still. Then a peace entered him that was incredible. For the first time in his life, he felt as though a heavy weight had been taken off of him. Then he noticed that his sweat-drenched garments had an absolutely hideous stench to them. Bil spent hours in the shower. It was at the exorcism that God saved him. When Rosemary came home she found a different man. But that frightened her even more. Not long after that, she plotted to take him to the holding tank for psychiatric observation. But God had a plan even in this.

Bil's doctor at the psychiatric facility was Dr. Clarence Jones. He had just accepted Christ and started coming to Calvary Chapel. One thing that impressed the doctor was that even under massive doses of the drug Stellazine, they could not in any way subdue Bil's excited proclamations about Christ. Indeed they became frightened of this powerful figure who kept announcing to them, "Jesus is coming!" This apparently had an effect on Dr. Jones. He even came to see me at Calvary Chapel, hoping to prove that agnosticism was the only viable option for "realists."

Dr. Jones is now a Messianic Jew. Soon after he had Bil released, he saw him at one of the Calvary Chapel services. Dr. Jones suddenly turned around to see a smiling and sane Bil Gallatin sitting right behind him. Then he announced to Bil, "Don't worry about the medical fees, I've got them covered."

RECOVERY, GROWTH, AND GUIDANCE

For seven years Bil Gallatin attended Calvary Chapel Costa Mesa, learning diligently. He couldn't seem to get enough. He exulted over the change in his life's destiny. His emotional scars in him slowly healed as he prayed fervently, worshiped, fellowshiped, joined the staff for a year as a carpenter, and led the evening Afterglow services. But by the summer of 1977, God had just about gotten Bil where He wanted him. He was being prepared for the task of pioneering Calvary Chapel back East.

For those who wonder how God "speaks" to individuals, Bil's experience of God's direction provides a clear example. Granted, we hear about counterfeits of this all the time, and cults are rife with false guidance. But that does not disprove the genuine leading of God. When I refer to divine guidance, I am not speaking about "new revelations" in the area of doctrines. It is clear that anything that calls itself revelatory truth "beyond" or "added to" Scripture is heresy. The canon of completed Scripture has indeed been given once and for all to all the saints. I am talking about God directly guiding our lives when He so chooses. To say that God cannot lead us these days is to put Him in a box. The Bible is loaded with very clear examples of God leading individuals, groups, and nations in particular situations. But the final test of God's genuine leading (as God pointed out to Moses in Deuteronomy chapter 18) is that the results are borne out in history. What God speaks, happens! In Bil's case, what looked impossible from a human perspective indeed took place.

First of all there came the inward nudges. Bil began to feel pulled toward the ministry. His impact at our Afterglow services was significant. In his heart there grew a strong desire to teach the Word of God. At the same time, Bil was feeling limited at Calvary Chapel in the daily routines of his carpentry work. There were other capacities in him on hold. Bil was pulling desperately at the bit.

Then the first arrow from God's quiver began to strike home. Bil was having a prayer meeting with two classmates from Calvary's first Shepherd School, Mike MacIntosh and Keith Ritter. Keith suddenly announced, "I have a vision from the Lord and it is about Bil." Keith described a pastoral scene out of picture-book New England. "I see a tall silo almost filled to the top with grain. It is surrounded by farm animals. I get the impression of a farm setting. There is also a carriage or covered wagon in the picture." Mike was given the interpretation. The silo represented Bil as the feeder of the animals, which stood for the flock of believers that God had waiting for him. Bil was almost full of "grain" and ready to feed. The location was in some farm territory outside of California, maybe out East.

One day, a month or so after this, Bil was working on our new parking lot. As clear and as certain as anything Bil had ever heard came a voice, "I want you to go to the Finger Lakes." Immediately Bil started to weep, because he knew it was from God. Bil had been to upstate New York as a young man, when his dad had lived in Rochester. The Finger Lakes were in upstate New York.

Rosemary was horrified. She became a Christian two years after Bil, but she didn't really want to leave California. If they were going to leave she wanted to make sure it was really God leading. She needed confirmation from Scripture. The next evening at Calvary Chapel's Thursday night service, a girl sitting in front of them, whom Rosemary knew, suddenly turned around and said, "This may seem strange, but I feel that the Lord is giving me a passage to share with you. It is Deuteronomy chapter eight."

It was Bil's fortieth birthday. Amazingly, the passage was addressed to Moses when he had turned forty. In it, God said to Moses that He had tested him those forty years, and was sending him into a land of hills, lakes, springs, wheat, and barley. That is the passage that convinced them. Bil was now certain that for him to resist God's clear indications to move to New York would be a clear case of spiritual disobedience. The case was closed the next morning when they woke up in their rented Newport Beach house to see the owner hammering a For Sale sign out front.

Three weeks later on July 7, 1977, (Bil notes the date as 7/7/77) Bil and Rosemary Gallatin arrived in upstate New York in a beat-up old Chevy containing two kids, all their worldly goods, and a German shepherd. Bil had eight-five cents in his pocket. They landed in Farmington and moved into a townhouse with a clear view of a solitary silo near them.

This marked the beginning of a new Calvary Chapel. And it was tough going at first. Among other divisive things, some locals said that Bil was a false prophet. These blows knocked the wind out of him time and again. Bil would call me occasionally and ask to come back. I told him to keep plowing. God then told Bil that if he would persevere for three years, the harvest would come. God gave Bil a passage in Zechariah about taking His people through the fire. And for three years they just barely scraped by. Bil couldn't even fall back on his construction skills since he was suffering from torn ligaments. When friends left food on Bil and Rosemary's porch, it was like Elijah being fed by the ravens.

But the three years passed. Bil's burgeoning Bible study moved into an empty train depot. It would seat 150. Bil was unnerved by the size of it. But a year later, in 1981, they were having two Sunday services. A year after that they expanded the rail depot so it could hold 250 a service. They immediately had to go to three services since more than 750 people were coming on Sunday mornings. Traffic was becoming a problem for local residents. It was finally when they went to five Sunday services that the heat was on for them to move.

Then Bil found the place, the town of Canandaigua. This Indian name means "chosen spot." On Route 332, on the Farmington border, Bil had often noticed a brand new skating rink that was not being used. It did not have enough people coming to make it financially viable, so it had been closed. In no time he purchased the 26,000-square-foot facility with no down payment!

Here was another example of the miracle of the harvest. Within three weeks of opening their thousand seat capacity new facility, they were forced to go to three services to make room for everyone. That was in 1984. Today, Bil has been able to start more spin-off churches in nearby Rochester and neighboring areas.

A stone's throw from the church stands a tall silo in the town of Farmington. History has borne out the vision that God provided at that prayer meeting. God's many proddings to get Bil Gallatin where he was called to minister have brought astounding results. Calvary Chapel has seen great harvest in upstate New York, where it already has become one of the largest churches in the region. And Bil is a deeply contented man. He has come a staggering distance from that kitchen floor, where he was set free by the power of God. Not even the wildest dreamer would have ventured to notion that such a man would one day be the humble, strong, and balanced pastor that God would use to build a church of thousands from scratch.

In 2003, Bil was called by the Lord to Switzerland. Since that time he has been in some 15 countries in Europe. He is motivated by his love for Jesus and a strong desire to see that the brethren in Europe are strengthened in God's Word.

While in Switzerland, a Bible study began in Basel and later in St. Gallen. Bil and his wife, Rosemary, will remain a vital part of CC Finger Lakes and keep their home in New York, enabling Bil to accept conference invitations all over the world.

J O E F O C H T

MEDITATING UNDERCOVER

In God's economy of purpose, it is ironic that the man he used to take Calvary Chapel to Philadelphia, a town famous for boxers, had hopes and dreams of his own. Joe Focht, a native of Philadelphia, had entered the Golden Gloves tournament in the late 1960's. This 6'1" aspiring athlete seemed to have it in sight to win the Gloves, when suddenly, during a fight, a spinal disk ruptured. Joe was trying to hit his opponent hard from an odd angle. He made an awkward twist and felt his back snap. He went down from the pain. Overnight he got sciatica so badly that he dragged his leg and had to wear a body brace for a while. That ended Joe's boxing hopes.

College had been another disappointment. In 1968, Joe went to Colorado State at Fort Collins for one meaningless semester, then dropped out. It seemed hollow. Issues of ultimate meaning overshadowed the significance of his classes. Joe had gone to please his dad, but that had shallow rewards as well. Joe, typical of his generation, was alienated from both his parents.

Later, after the accident, he moved back home and felt like an alien. Plus, because of his injury, he no longer had much in common with his old group of athletic friends.

Joe started to look for physical healing for his back. He tried hatha yoga and seemed to get better. That led to other forms of yoga as he threw himself into classes under his new Indian guru, Amrith Desai. Joe had a new circle of friends. Soon he was trying LSD with some of them. He then combined LSD and meditation. Then he added vegetarianism to his regimen and joined a rock-and-roll band. Within a year or two, his mother was virtually crying in despair. Joe was pale, had long hair, and when he sat down to talk with his dad, his dad would leave a half-hour later not understanding a word that his son had said. What had been a communication gap between Joe and his parents now took on cosmic dimensions.

In 1971, when Guru Maharaji was popular, Joe went to a New York City auditorium to hear him speak. Then Joe spent two days in a devotee's house waiting in line to be initiated by the boy guru. The experience did not impress Joe, but he began to practice Maharaji's technique of meditating under a blanket.

One day in the spring of 1972 when Joe was in meditation, he envisioned himself running along an open field. He sensed a heavy pressure coming down on his back. Fear hit Joe as he sensed he was being pursued by some large creature with wings. When the wing flapping came close enough to hear, Joe had the distinct impression that the creature was very evil. Suddenly he fell down in the field. He called on the name of Maharaji for help and nothing happened. Something in Joe knew that he should call on the name of Jesus. He did and immediately the creature disappeared. Joe filed this away in his mind.

THE PRESENCE OF CHRIST

In the fall of 1972 Joe's rock band rented a summer estate called Innisfree Estate at Skinner's Falls, Pennsylvania. By now, Joe's mystical pursuit was obsessive. He and his best friend, Harris, moved to the estate a month early before the rest of the band arrived. They brought hundreds of pounds of grain to eat along with wild roots and herbs that they cooked. They bathed in the cold river and spent half the night meditating. The estate had a decadent feel of opulence.

At three a.m. one morning Joe and Harris got into an argument. Joe had been reading the Bible from time to time, and Harris wanted to leave it behind arguing, "The Bible is against everything we've been doing." But Harris agreed to look at it one time. They threw the Bible open and their eyes fell on 1 Corinthians 11. They had been doing their meditation under blankets again. The passage read, in effect, 'Never pray with a veil over your head.' This statement made an impact on them.

Joe describes that moment: "The presence of the Lord stepped right into the room. It was tangible. There was the overwhelming sensation of a Person—not just a power or a force. I knew it was God in Christ. Harris felt it too. The Presence was so holy that I just hung my head. I couldn't lift it. We both started weeping. All of our previous ideas about finding nirvana were flushed out of our minds. Jesus was alive, and truly God in and of Himself. He washed all the junk away. We wept and wept as we felt His awesomely holy Presence.

"That was it, the end of the road, of our search. We were converted. As I used to say, 'You know when you know that you know.' We were sealed with the Holy Spirit in the early hours of that morning in September 1972."

When the band arrived Joe rehearsed with them and studied the Bible on the side. He read a verse that said everyone should remain in the situation he was in when God called him. So Joe toured with the band for three more years. But by 1975 the temptations on the road had gotten the better of Joe's faith and he realized after continual backsliding with drugs and women that God had better things for him.

CHRISTIAN CULTS AND FALSE TEACHINGS

Joe's zeal for Christianity, plus his guilt over backsliding with the band, opened him up to being spiritually seduced. Joe was soon hooked up with one of many unbalanced Christian cults that have sprung up in our time. A girl on the West Coast wrote him about the "extra-anointed" brand of Christianity she had found. With its extreme demands on its disciples, how could it be anything but real?

For a while the Children of God claimed to be the only true Christians. The same was true of the Vine House, or the Apostolic Seven, the Jim Jones sect, The Way International, and so on. These groups rarely converted anyone, but honed in on people who came to Christ through other ministries, stealing them away. This is a perfect illustration of the parable of the sower in which the devil's agents try to steal away the new believers. To groups such as these their "new revelation", abstinence, and sacrificial lifestyle prove to them that they are the only true Christians on earth.

The girl who wrote Joe was a member of Jim Durkin's Lighthouse Ranch. In the end Joe spent four years on the West Coast, in Jim Durkin's Shepherding movement. Durkin is a self-appointed apostle. Those in the group come to a point where they passively accept any guidance they are given until they can barely make the simplest decisions for themselves. Joe lived in communal houses, worked, and gave all his earnings to the ministry. Like many cultic groups, they worked to the point of exhaustion, ate poorly, and slept poorly in a communal setting. They were under constant submission to elders, whether they traveled and played music for the community or worked at other jobs.

When Joe was at the San Diego commune of Gospel Outreach in 1976 and 1977, he attended Mike MacIntosh's rapidly growing Calvary Chapel Horizon Fellowship. As he saw what God was doing at Horizon, he kept wondering why their own small fellowship of thirty never grew beyond that number. When Joe attended Horizon, he was invariably nourished by the teaching and the joy of the fellowship. But it still took several years for Joe to understand the difference.

Joe had to ask permission from the elders to marry a woman named Cathy. The elders had chosen another man for her to marry, but finally gave him permission. Joe and Cathy spent two more years with Gospel Outreach in Oregon, Seattle, and San Diego. They became depleted spiritually. Not only was there no experience of spiritual joy for them, but Cathy kept getting sick. She began to battle several skin cancers and other diseases. Meanwhile, after all of their sacrifices for this group, they were given no encouragement or help for Cathy. Joe became bitter. They moved in with Cathy's parents in Whittier, California, in 1979. Joe felt like a failure.

RESTORATION AND MINISTRY

By the time Joe and Cathy left Jim Durkin's movement, burnout, exhaustion, cynicism, and disillusionment had taken a terrible toll on their souls. Something had been robbed from them. Joe needed a time of healing as much as he did when he left the band. As a couple, Joe and Cathy started attending various Calvary Chapels. They left Cathy's parents' house for six months and went to San Diego where they continued going to Horizon Fellowship. God told Joe during this period, after all his exhaustion from striving to be in the ministry, "*I don't want you in the ministry. I want the ministry to be in you.*"

By 1980 they moved back to Whittier and on Thursday nights came to hear me teach at Costa Mesa. Joe felt led to go back to the East Coast. I called him into my office and prayed for him, sensing that good things lay ahead for him there. They moved to Philadelphia in 1981. By November of that year, Joe had found a place to begin a Bible study in Northeast Philadelphia, a catering hall. After six months a hundred people were attending.

In November 1984, Calvary Chapel of Philadelphia moved to their present location, a facility that was formerly a meter factory. They have four services on Sundays with over 12,000 adults and children in attendance. Joe is also on the radio five days a week. Like Bil Gallatin, Joe never asks for money and he never has advertised his ministry. In fact Joe and Bil have never asked for a salary. The elders had to press it upon them. Joe was once told by a skeptical local man, "That's why I trust you. You are not out for money like so many others."

Joe comments that it has been slow going on the East Coast. But once you convert someone you reach into his community. Unlike the West Coast, there are 200-year-old Italian and German neighborhoods in Philadelphia. These people are street smart and, frankly, wary of most things coming out of California. So it is a tough task to prove that you are genuine. Joe's situation is remarkably different from that of Jon Courson in Oregon. It is interesting to see that no one formula works, but that different fellowships seem to find innovative approaches as God directs.

Joe Focht and Bil Gallatin organize joint seasonal trips to Israel for members of their churches. Bil and Joe minister and teach on tour while they refresh one another's ministerial vision. They first became friends when they were roommates during my 1981 tour to Israel for Calvary Chapel pastors. They shared their backgrounds together, laughing and exulting over what God has done in their lives. Meanwhile, at a fellowship for pastors' wives in California, Cathy and Rosemary were randomly assigned as roommates and soon became close friends.

The stories of Bil and Joe plainly illustrate that when God moves in our lives, without our hindrance, doubt, resistance, or manipulation, He can achieve astounding things. It is always greater than any of our own ambitions or visions for what is possible in our lives.

Many times people look at Calvary Chapel as something that might work in California (where almost anything goes) but wonder if it would work in the East, where things are supposedly different. They wonder if the God-given principles that work on the West Coast would be successful in other parts of the country. Well, we have observed that wherever these principles have been applied, God has blessed. Though people may be different as far as cultural backgrounds go, there is no difference in their common thirst for the truth and for God. At Calvary Chapel these young men have been learning how to bring the Living Water to a thirsty world. And they have seen the same results—nationwide.

CHAPTER 12

MIKE MacINTOSH
NEITHER DEAD NOR ALIVE

It was evident to the audience of three thousand that this tanned, healthy-looking speaker who stood before them, in his late thirties, radiating exuberant good cheer, was not only "fully clothed and in his right mind" but was now a role model of success because Jesus had changed him.

But in the 1960s he had said, "I thought part of my head was missing. When I looked into the mirror, I saw half my face missing at times. For two years I walked around believing that when that gun went off only inches from my head, my brains were blown out. I figured it was only by some bizarre fluke of nature that I was able to exist like that. It was terrifying, and there wasn't a thing in the world I could do about it. I lived in a gray shadow-world—I felt neither dead nor alive. I appeared to be stuck in a plane of consciousness that the world of modern science had not fully accounted for."

The speaker was Mike MacIntosh, and he was recounting the story of his pilgrimage out of an abyss. He had wandered through a certain kind of hell relegated to a small number of partiers in the '60s—the ones who crashed on "Owsley Blue Cheers" and "Yellows" and who never fully came back after the trip ended. At the end of his wild, reckless dive into chaos, Mike MacIntosh ended up seeking counseling for the next 17 months. The prospect for any meaningful kind of life at all for him was almost nil.

The '60s generation showed us that America had not yet run out of new frontiers. In the '50s the only things that seemed to dazzle with adventure were far beyond the reach of the average person. The promise of space colonization was still in the future. Historians pointed backward in time to illustrate the last of America's new frontiers—valleys of virgin forest, crystal-clear streams and lakes never seen before by civilized men stretching out before them, rippling in nature's silences.

It was easy to romanticize this distant past. Life was inhaled in a gigantic breath. Both the sense of joy and the potential for disaster were vivid in those days. Everything was new. By comparison, going to the bowling alley on Friday nights in the mid-1950s seemed dull and pedestrian.

By the '50s, the romance and adventure that come from being on the historical edge could only be found in books or the local movie house. America was so stable and its boundaries so fully explored that many, especially among the youth culture, grew restless.

When the '60s arrived that restlessness sprang into action. Popular musicians like Bob Dylan, Frank Zappa, and others started telling the older generation that they were trivial people from a trivial world doomed to extinction in the coming revolution. This uprising would be fueled by a change of consciousness, an anarchy of belief and morals. Indeed a new frontier had been discovered— mind-altering drugs. Soon the social revolution of the '60s would change the face of America. Newness and adventure were back on the horizon, but with a price tag that few could have anticipated.

It is interesting to walk through Berkeley's People's Park today, over twenty-five years after the psychedelic revolution. The old gurus have quieted. Instead there are squatter groups in the park— the mutterers and twitchers who had been the youth of the '60s are now street people. The yuppie generation at Cal Berkeley is career-oriented. They look with disdain at these "has-beens"—the early experimenters with LSD who burned the flag and dropped out. The yuppies have shelved the quest for higher truth and are working instead to get their careers established. And if they do get "high," now it is strictly for pleasure.

Not only has the heyday of the '60s generation passed, but the excesses of their youth have caught up with them. Many are now welfare cases, cared for by the very system they tried to destroy. They are unable to contribute to society or even pay their own way. When they were at the pinnacle of youthful energy, tanned, smiling, and getting high in the California sun, I bet that if they had been given a glimpse of how they would turn out they would have screamed in horror, thrown their pills and reefers into the Pacific, and questioned their own dreams.

Some of them did this, of course. They saw something down below, a glimpse of hell, if you will, that made them stop in their tracks. Mike MacIntosh was not the proverbial long-haired hippie, but rather he was one of the many typical conservative, middle-class party boys of that era. He also escaped the inferno of hell by the grace of God.

His narration in the auditorium in Maui was a testimony to days long gone. "I was in Yucca Valley at four o'clock in the morning chanting my TM (transcendental meditation) mantra. Below was a white-domed building. Some friends told me that it was a space machine that gave off electromagnetic pulses, and would take me back in time. Around the side of the hill nearby was a small airport. A UFO was due to arrive anytime."

Little wonder Mike wanted to board a UFO. His day-to-day world of 1969 left much to be desired. At twenty-four years of age his marriage was already beyond salvaging. His wife had fled with the kids. A spaceman for a father was not what she had in mind. He was thousands of dollars in debt to people he had attempted to cunningly hustle. He was about to be fired from work.

Describing his own descent into the abyss, Mike may have struck a chord of familiarity with those in that auditorium in Hawaii.

"One night I was left off at a party. After partying for a few hours, someone gave me some type of drug causing my speech and vision to blur rapidly, and I was becoming more and more paranoid every second. Everything became evidence of a conspiracy. Unfortunately there was plenty of evidence around. Ron, one of the guys at the party, looked like he was on the floor loading what appeared to be a hand-gun. I knew I was overdosing, so I asked for someone to take me to the hospital."

Ron shoved another bullet into the chamber of the revolver. "You're okay," he responded in a disgusted tone. "No problem."

Mike continued, "At a sign from Ron, I thought I felt those in the room grabbing me. They took off my shoes, socks, and shirt. Tied my hands behind my back. Then they tied a cloth bag over my head. I knew I was going to die. I saw 'spirit forms' floating by and I called out to them wondering if they were God or knew God. Among them was Maharishi who had promised that for one hundred and thirty-four dollars he could take me to God."

"I thought they pushed me to the floor and said they were going to kill me. Then I felt the barrel of the revolver pressed against my head. Suddenly I heard a deafening explosion. A forty-five pistol exploding only inches from your head is devastating. My head was gone; I knew it. My brains had been blown out. In truth it was either a blank or they fired at the wall, but to me that was it. The problem was that this perception of my brains being blown out stayed with me for over two years—an experience, I've since learned, that others have had."

Instability is a kind of hell. It is lonely; it is terrifying. In many ways, it is an alienation from all things. A person finds himself cut off from people, then finally reality itself.

Sherwood Wirt, author of For the Love of Mike, describes this moment:

"It was a beautiful February day in southern California. Mockingbirds were singing and the blossoms were on the peach trees, but for Michael MacIntosh life had lost its beauty. He knew he had hit bottom. The easy charm, the puckish, fun-loving demeanor had failed him. Not often had Michael been reduced to tears—once when his older brother, David, slammed into a telephone pole and was killed; once when he broke up with a high school sweetheart; and once, most agonizingly, when his wife, Sandra, moved out with little Melinda. But on this Sunday morning, Michael cried because he was in a holding tank, locked in the mental ward of a hospital with some strange-looking characters. And he was not getting out."

But that night as he shared his story, this young man by God's grace and healing had become the pastor of perhaps the largest church in San Diego, Horizon Christian Fellowship. It had grown to 5,000 attendees, and Mike was a popular speaker. He would soon appear on national television, giving his testimony at the huge 1985 Billy Graham Crusade in Anaheim. Not bad for a previous party boy trapped in an Orange County holding tank. There was no disputing the fact that Mike had not only been transformed by Christ, but now lived an enviably productive life.

Frankly, I never cease to be amazed at this miracle myself. I well remember the night in April of 1970, at Calvary Chapel Costa Mesa, when Mike stood up and finally came forward to dedicate his life to Christ. He certainly blended in with the sea of youth in bare feet and long hair that we always welcomed, just as they were. Christ would have done no less. As the church leaders laid hands and prayed for him, Mike felt God's divine love shower down upon him. He no longer held any grudges and the chips on his shoulder were gone.

Yet when Mike and I talked later, I frankly wondered whether he would ever come back down to earth. For, during those turbulent years of the late '60s and early '70s, we had thousands of young people like Mike who had come to Calvary Chapel from the 60's culture. Not everyone made it, so deeply had they fallen in their search for spiritual reality. Many thought they had found fulfillment in psychedelics. They felt that their mandate was to create a world of love and peace by getting everyone stoned at the same time. This was their own version of heaven on earth.

Woodstock was to be a dramatic demonstration to the world of the utopia possible when masses of people get stoned together, drop their "head-games," and just "groove" on rock music. True, a few had fun. But there remained the reality of drug overdoses, orgies, rapes, fights, and stealing to sully the anticipated picture of perfect harmony and brotherly love. To make matters worse, the food system barely held for the three day event. By the time the horde of over a half-million left "Woodstock Nation" in upstate New York, the once verdant fields were flattened, and tons of trash blew in the wind. Rain had created a massive field of sludge, which the crowd danced in as the rock festival wore into its third day. Perhaps prophetically, the sludge was a metaphor for what was to come.

Within a matter of months, a second utopian experiment was under way. The Rolling Stones had a massive concert at Altamont, California. But this event became a horrible nightmare for the thousands in attendance. Pandemonium set in. There was even more violence, including rapes and beatings. And this time there were killings. The Hell's Angels, serving as "police," had stabbed a man, setting off a dangerously chaotic scene. It happened while Mick Jagger was singing "Sympathy for the Devil." The Hell's Angels stormed to the front to kill the first troublemaker and make an example of him to the rather wimpy "flower people" who were shoving toward the stage. When the fellow produced a switchblade, it was reason enough for the Angels to crush him. By the end of the Altamont concert, the hippie utopian dream of universal brotherhood and love was shattered. They had touted Rousseau's ideal of the "noble savage." They believed that man, unfettered by civilization, was basically good and innocent. But what people saw in themselves and others while on drugs was a magnitude of sheer perversity, cruelty, hardness, and selfishness that was terrifying. This reality signaled the end of the hippie era.

After Altamont, disillusioned and broken, many of the victims of the drug culture showed up on our steps at Calvary Chapel. We heard some incredible stories. Many of these kids had so fried their minds with various powerful substances that they would never recover from the damage. They had gone too far into a world of fantasy and could not find their way back to reality. Some of them injected almost anything into their veins (including peanut butter) in search of a new kind of "high."

So for the first six months, as Mike MacIntosh would share his fantasy world, we wondered if he was one of the permanent casualties. But gradually we saw changes that were encouraging signs to us. We saw God begin to restore the years that the locusts had eaten.

Within months of his conversion, twenty-six-year-old Mike, who had been floating from house to house, or living in a shack at Newport Beach, chose to move into one of our Christian-run communes. Its real ministry was to offer newly converted but still rootless youth a place that they could call home.

Youth who had been bound by drugs gained freedom in Jesus. They worked together in an environment of love—true love, Christ's love. They worked hard, studied God's Word, learned to abide in the Holy Spirit, and grew in character as they faced the responsibility of sticking to decisions. This meant moral restraint and self-control. If they had squandered years in reckless abandon, old habits were overcome. The smile of innocence did return. Many scraped, painted, and rebuilt the group house. Others went out and got responsible jobs and put money back into the house. They paid their debts and learned to face the responsibilities of adulthood.

Clearly God was the power behind this radical change. The house community prayed, extended themselves unselfishly to others, and studied their Redeemer within the pages of the Bible. This was anything but cheap escapism for youth who had grown accustomed to the easy life of hedonism, when they could do what they wanted at any time. Meanwhile, Mike MacIntosh grew like a fern in a greenhouse. He was becoming a gifted leader and teacher, as he assumed more and more responsibilities over the house ministry.

But there were still tangible reminders of Mike's failed past. Sandy, Mike's ex-wife, was back in town. When he first met her, he charmed her with every image and facade he could, inventing one incredible story after another. Even though Mike was a high school dropout, he read passages from high-sounding books to seem knowledgeable to this college coed. Among other things, he claimed to be a med student from the University of Oregon.

On a whim and after only three weeks of knowing Mike, Sandy agreed to drive to Las Vegas and marry him. It was a twelve-dollar civil ceremony. They took their vows in blue jeans and bare feet. Soon enough Mike's glitter tarnished. Sandy finally saw the utter contradiction of his life. This pretty and devoted girl had been forced to drop out of college to support Mike and their little girl while he surfed and got stoned. It was too much. So, pregnant for the second time, she fled back to the luxurious home of her affluent parents back East. Their doubts about this social outcast had been proven right.

Of course, if you know the whole story of Mike MacIntosh, then there is another side to consider. His childhood in Oregon was a sad tale of a youth with promise being shattered by the sledgehammer of circumstance. There was a time, in his sunnier, more innocent years, when Mike made straight A's and was a star baseball player. He excelled in the Cub Scouts, had lots of friends, and by early high school was voted "student of the year." Mike, in those days, was willing to trust just about everyone. He had a cherubic smile that lit up a room like a sunrise. Sensitivity and vulnerability were in his nature. And even though life had always been tough for Mike, he had always been able to rise above it, looking on the bright side. He kept this up through the hungry and uncertain years of a repeatedly broken home and the poverty that accompanied it.

But eventually the world beat Mike down. His allotment of misfortune seemed completely out of proportion to that of other people. Everything that ever meant anything to him was taken away bit by bit until he felt he had nothing. First, he had to cope with the distant alcoholic father he never knew. When he finally did get the father-figure he had yearned for (the third man his mother had married), even this was taken away. The stepfather left. This was traumatic, but the final blow for Mike came when his older brother, his role model and hero figure, was killed in a car accident. Suddenly, life had the bitter taste of a cosmic joke. And, if life is a joke, then you treat it like a joke. Mike dropped out of high school, joined the Army for a while, and then went on his solitary pilgrimage down the road. By the time he met Sandy, he was a seasoned beach bum who knew how to manipulate and hustle people to get what he wanted. With no hope for the future, he learned to live for the brief pleasures of the moment.

Now Sandy was back with her family trying to finish college, this time without Mike around to spoil her life. But Mike still had the legal right as a father to see his child. And, now that he was a Christian, it was hard for Sandy not to notice the change in him. But it seemed too good to be true. Mike had cried wolf too many times. Sandy watched him with a critical eye. And she kept seeing that the change in him was real, that it had substance. Finally, without him manipulating her, she went to a Calvary Chapel beach concert and that did it. Sandy saw the same Spirit of love in the Christians who packed the beach that she had seen in Mike. When an invitation to accept Christ was given, Sandy, in tears, knelt to give her life to Christ. I have no doubt that God knew that Mike needed Sandy, for his life and for his ministry.

The day I had the privilege of remarrying Mike and Sandy, with little blonde Mindi serving as flower girl, the tears of joy flowed freely for we knew that God's restoration was complete. In fact, the wedding had to be stopped right in the middle because so many people were sobbing, including the bride and groom. That touching moment is hard to describe.

As Mike developed during the house community era and beyond, it was obvious that he had leadership ability and was an excellent communicator. His track record in retail sales showed that he was responsible and hardworking. He was also very interested in music, so when we started Maranatha! Music with our first album, a demo featuring all of our groups, Mike became our first distributor. In those days, he would fill the trunk of his car with albums and travel throughout California entreating the Christian bookstores to stock this new kind of Christian music. It worked and sales started to take off. As Mike proved his abilities, we turned Maranatha! Music over to him. But Mike's first love remained his desire to communicate his faith to audiences in an evangelistic context. The music ran a close second only because he could see that it captured the attention of the audience and could create an opening for direct evangelism.

As director of Maranatha! Music, Mike was also the road manager for various bands. When they were on tour, he used the break time between sets to come out and give his testimony or share some burden on his heart. Many made commitments to Jesus. These opportunities to share Jesus Christ publicly began to be those prime-time moments for which Mike longed. He knew by the eyes of the audience that he was getting through to them for Christ. By the time he traveled with a band and various musicians to Manila to play before 15,000 people each night, Mike was getting impressive results as a communicator of the gospel of Christ.

In 1975, some students came to me from San Diego State, asking if I could send someone to their area to start a church. They had been driving up each week for the services at Calvary Chapel. Immediately I thought of Mike, knowing that he was God's choice for this task. Mike had already been commuting weekly to San Diego to teach at their rapidly expanding Bible study at the Hospitality House at Balboa Park.

Yet when I told Mike that I was going to give him a month's vacation with pay, and that during that month he was to move to San Diego to start a Calvary Chapel, he was surprised. He had come to look upon me as the father he had never had, and it was, for him, like a father telling his son to leave the nest. However, because he loved me as a dad he moved to San Diego without hesitation. He accepted my guidance without question and committed himself to work as hard as possible to make me proud of my son in the faith.

In just a few months' time Mike invited me down to speak before his Wednesday night Bible study, which by then was meeting in a large church auditorium in Linda Vista. And indeed I could not have been more proud and thrilled as I saw the hundreds of shining young faces jamming that auditorium beyond its capacity (they were among the countless converts to Jesus Christ from Mike's ministry). Sunday services were running well over a thousand people.

In less than a year Mike consulted us about purchasing the North Park Theater, where Burns and Allen and Sophie Tucker once played. This grand theater was needed to seat the thousands of young people who were showing up. We helped them purchase the theater, which was soon beautifully refurbished. On Sundays it became common place to see crowds streaming out onto University Avenue, after sitting through a packed service filled with contemporary worship and the solid teaching of God's Word.

At North Park the music was electric. And, when Mike came out to speak, you could hear a pin drop. Rolled up in this communicator was a virtuoso of humor, irony, pointed insight, and endless stories. He was spontaneous as he ad-libbed, or mimed, or became the comic, making fun of himself and human nature. Beneath it all was a vibrant awareness of God's grace and love, all of which he brought to bear on Scripture. And no one could seem to get enough of it. Here was a man who at different times knew what it was like to be a surfer, a tripper, and a yuppie. He had done it all, yet what mattered most to him was the love of Jesus. When he spoke it was with the authority of someone who knew what he was talking about and believed deeply. Sometimes he was in a colorful T-shirt, other times he wore a coat and tie, but beneath it all was a deadly serious concern to be obedient to Jesus and care for the souls before him.

Mike then started a school of evangelism and began to train hundreds of young people to share their faith. He also began to give birth to other churches in San Diego County as he encouraged key people in leadership to spread out from the home church and start their own. If you ask Mike, he will tell you that he is called to be an evangelist as well as a Bible expositor. He might even tell you that he has a secret yearning to be on the road speaking at evangelistic rallies.

Today every major community in San Diego County has a Horizon Calvary Chapel, and the home church, Horizon Christian Fellowship, has moved to an enormous school complex that houses an auditorium, a cafeteria, tennis courts, basketball courts, a gym, classrooms, and a bookstore. Mike is on radio and television, his ministry has published a widely distributed periodical called Horizon International Magazine, the numerous evangelistic missions of his school of evangelism to various foreign countries have had far-reaching effects, and God's use of Mike as the proclamation evangelist in up to four major campaigns each year is a tribute to Jesus' working through him to bring others to salvation. The work of his ministry is highlighted in Dr. Elmer Towns' book, 10 of Today's Most Innovative Churches.

Of all the Calvary Chapel affiliate pastors, I think that the life of Mike MacIntosh shows Jesus' greatest healing and deliverance from the widest range of cultural depravities to beset the '60s generation. Mike had been stained with such depravities as instability, drugs, shattered ethics and morals, as well as divorce both in his parents' marriage and in his own. I have seen Mike MacIntosh change from a seemingly hopeless beach bum, mental case to a man who loves Jesus, a man who is sane, dedicated, and devout. He is now a responsible husband, father, Christian leader, pastor, and evangelist, whose far-reaching ministry has become a phenomenon. If this does not show that Jesus is real enough to satisfy the skeptic, I am not sure what does!

Let us now prayerfully seek the help of the Holy Spirit to understand the simple biblical principles that Mike and these other men learned at Calvary Chapel, things that I had to learn through years of experience in struggle and failure. Are these truths transferable? Can others, even without formal Bible training, follow these principles and develop large and effective ministries? Hundreds of strong churches resoundingly say, "YES"!

Presently the ministry of Horizon that extends both nationally and internationally includes an innovative, growing church ministry, a school of evangelism, a 4-year college, and approximately 100 churches and parachurch organizations that have emerged from Horizon San Diego. Horizon holds evangelistic Festivals of Life in the United States and other countries, and works with several orphanages internationally. Horizon USA is the relief arm of the ministry, serving in New York City after September 11, 2001, the 2003 San Diego fires, and Hurricane Katrina in the Gulf Coast in 2005. The Horizon school system spans kindergarten through high school, serving over 1,500 students.

All of these ministries reflect the heart of Mike MacIntosh's vision of winning a person for Jesus Christ, discipling a person in Jesus Christ, and sending a person for Jesus Christ. They also bless me as his spiritual dad, for they reflect my heart as well.

PRINCIPLES OF GROWTH

Many churches are built around the personality of the pastor and as a result the work cannot be duplicated and the concepts are not transferable. Trying to imitate another person's personality is never successful. God has made us all unique individuals and His Spirit anoints us according to our own individual characteristics.

Many times a pastor who is anxious to see church growth makes the mistake of going to large, successful churches, looking at their programs, and watching the way the minister relates to his people. Then the pastor tries to copy the program and the personality. And it just doesn't work.

It is true that God does work through personalities. They play a very important part in the way we relate to people. But because Calvary Chapel has been built on principles rather than personalities, the principles are transferable and work in all varieties of personalities. Through following these simple steps Calvary Chapel pastors have found tremendously successful ministries. Let me share them with you.

When I first began in the ministry I served in a denomination whose main emphasis was evangelism. This was reflected by the fact that the first bit of information required on my monthly report was the number of people saved. The next box was for the number of people baptized. I had heard so often that the primary purpose of the Church was the evangelization of the world, thus every sermon that I preached was somehow brought around to evangelism and the appeal made for people to accept Jesus Christ as their Lord and Savior.

My greatest frustration would come when I would prepare what I felt to be a powerful evangelistic sermon that would surely convert the most hardened sinner. And when I would arrive at church to my dismay there was not a single sinner in the whole congregation.

As I would sit on the platform looking over the congregation, I knew them all by first name, so I knew there wasn't a sinner in the house. During the song service I'd pray that God would somehow send sinners in and when my prayers were not answered I had to preach my evangelistic sermon to the saints. There was no hope of conversions. As a general rule I would add a few points in which I would castigate those in the congregation for their failures to be the kind of witnesses that the Lord wanted them to be. I told them if they were serving the Lord and were doing what God wanted them to do they would have brought some of their neighbors along to hear the Word of God and to be saved. I would begin to beat the sheep because they were not effectively reproducing or witnessing for Jesus Christ.

My heart aches when I think of those early days of my ministry, how I was creating guilt-ridden, frustrated believers. They were guilt-ridden because what I was saying was correct. They weren't being the kind of witnesses that they should be for Christ. Their lives weren't measuring up to biblical standards. They were frustrated because they desired to live victorious lives, but they just didn't know how because their pastor was emphasizing evangelism rather than feeding the Body of Christ.

This was the first lesson. Traditionally I felt that the primary purpose of the Church was the evangelization of the world. But biblically, Paul in Ephesians 4 tells us that the primary purpose of the Church is to build up the Body of Christ to perfect the saints for the work of the ministry. The church exists to bring people into a maturity and a unity of the faith so that they would no longer be as babes but might fully develop in Christ Jesus. With my constant emphasis on the repentance from dead works and the doctrines of baptism, I had failed to bring the people into a fully matured relationship with the Lord and they stayed in a state of spiritual infancy.

The second lesson in my own ministry came about in an interesting way.

My messages were topical, taken from Scriptures throughout the Bible. There was no consistent pattern in my preaching. One week my text might be from Matthew, the next week from Isaiah, the following week from Revelation, and the following from Genesis. I would share whatever topic happened to interest me that week or whatever Scripture might have just spoken to me. The most difficult part of the ministry at that time was finding a text from which to preach. I would find myself reading a book of the Bible until some Scripture sort of stood out in my mind and then I would develop from that text my message. I found that I had about two years of good topical sermons before I ran out of ideas and so my first few pastorates were of two years' duration. After I had exhausted my two years' of texts, I would seek a transfer to another church. This continued until we lived in Huntington Beach. We were coming close to the end of our two years and it was time to move again, but a problem had developed. We had fallen in love with Huntington Beach! We enjoyed living there and our little girl had now started school. We did not want to leave.

Suddenly I was under pressure to find more texts and more sermons. About this time I was reading the book *The Apostle John* by Griffith Thomas. In one of the chapters he had outlined studies on 1 John. As I studied those outlines I found that they were excellent sermon material and there were approximately forty of them. I decided that if I taught through the book of 1 John on Sunday mornings, we could spend another year in this community that we had come to love. I bought several commentaries on 1 John and began an exhaustive study of the epistle. I expanded the outline studies of Griffith Thomas and we spent a year on 1 John.

The interesting thing is that during this year our church experienced greater growth than we had ever seen before. We also had more conversions and more baptisms than we had ever experienced in the past. The people were suddenly filled with joy in their walk with Christ, they were experiencing greater power over sin, and they had a greater assurance of their salvation. Of course, these are the three reasons why John wrote the epistle and we are told that God's Word will not return void but will accomplish the purposes for which it was sent. Inasmuch as this epistle was sent to bring the believers into the fullness of joy, freedom from sin, and assurance of their salvation, God's Word did its work within their lives.

And so I learned the second lesson. Expositional teaching is stronger than topical teaching for feeding the flock.

At the end of the year we still did not want to leave Huntington Beach. Having developed the style of teaching straight through a book, I decided to take the book of Romans next, which a seminary professor had told us would transform any church. I bought as many commentaries as I could find on the book of Romans, and spent two years teaching on it. During this time the church doubled. The work of the Spirit in the hearts of the people was electrifying as they and I personally discovered the grace of God and began to relate to God in a new way. It was about this time that I purchased a new Halley's Bible Handbook. (I was always giving mine away to the new converts.)

On the flyleaf I saw a notation that said the most important page in the book was page 814. So I turned to that page to find out what Mr. Halley felt was the most important thing. There was the simple suggestion that every church have a congregational plan of Bible reading, and that the pastor's sermon be from the part of the Bible read the past week. I had never taken the people through the whole Bible. As a matter of fact I had never sat down to read the Bible straight through.

So I incorporated the third lesson. I decided that I would start the congregation reading the whole Bible, ten chapters a week, and that my sermon would come out of the chapters that they had read. I have been following this practice now for many years and have seen people in the church, for the first time in their lives, read the Bible all the way through.

These two transitions–from topical messages to expository teaching, and to working straight through the Bible—have taught me some very fascinating things. Number one, I came to the realization that during the years of my topical ministry I did not have a true biblical emphasis in my preaching. Though I preached every sermon from the Scriptures, my preaching was not biblically balanced. The Scriptures tell of God's part and of man's part in salvation. The majority of the topical sermons that I preached were emphasizing man's responsibility. My sermons exhorted the people to pray, to witness, to commit their lives to serving the Lord.

But when you get into a book of the Bible and continue straight through, you find there is a greater emphasis on what God has done for man than what man should be doing for God. In a sense, through the topical sermons, I was emphasizing what we should be doing for God in order that God might respond to us. I was making man the initiator and God the respondent. For instance, if you give, God will give back to you, measured out, pressed down, running over. If you praise, you will be blessed with a sense of His presence, for He inhabits the praises of His people. If you will win souls, you will be wise and shine as the stars forever.

But now I learned that God is always the initiator so His part is always first. Take the book of Ephesians as an example. Paul spends the first three chapters of the epistle telling the church what God had done for them. He prefaces this section with these words: "Blessed be the God and Father of our Lord Jesus Christ, who has blessed us with every spiritual blessing in the heavenly places in Christ ." And then he lists the glorious spiritual blessings and benefits that we have from God. It is not until he gets to chapter four that he deals with human responsibility by exhorting the people to walk worthy of this calling wherewith they were called.

God was the initiator and now Paul exhorted man to respond to God. I found that when people began to discover who God is and all that God has done, they were eager to respond to God and did not have to be pushed or exhorted to pray or to serve. Now they were volunteering their service and their time. They could not do enough for the Lord as they came to the recognition of what He had done for them.

The second thing I learned from these lessons was that evangelism is the natural byproduct of a healthy church. When, in the early years of my ministry, I placed an emphasis constantly on the people going out and winning someone to Jesus Christ, the numbers that were coming to the Lord were very small. When I began to feed the Body of Christ with the Word of God, we had more conversions and baptisms in the first year than we had had in any previous year of our ministry. And as the people continued to grow, the numbers the next year doubled, and it just continued to go that way because the people now were strong and spiritually healthy.

Then we happened on the third interesting change to come out of these experiences. Christmas and Easter Sundays were bedlam. There were always so many people coming to Sunday school and to church that the facilities couldn't hold them. Thus, those who would come only once or twice a year would come during the most trying circumstances, which didn't really encourage them to come back on a regular basis.

To deal with the problem of overcrowded rooms and the confusion in general, we decided that on Christmas and Easter we would not have Sunday school followed by church, but would have Sunday school for the children and Sunday morning service for the adults simultaneously. We had found in the past that many people would come to Sunday school and leave before church and thus never hear the Gospel. So by bringing the adults together for teaching they had greater opportunity to receive the Gospel message.

Everyone loved it so much we continued the practice year-round. We also discovered that with the children being taught on their own grade levels and not being present in the sanctuary during the service heightened the attention level of the adults considerably. They were able to understand and absorb much more without the distractions of their children around them. As the morning service and Sunday school ran concurrently, I became, in a sense, the teacher of the adult class that happened to be held in the main sanctuary. Later on we slipped naturally into the fourth lesson: double services. This worked out even better because then those who were teaching Sunday school could attend the next service, and it provided us with a lot more volunteers for the Sunday school program.

In going to double services we found that a smaller auditorium and smaller facilities were able to accommodate twice the number of people. So when we were in our building program we deliberately built the auditorium and facility with the intention of having double services. We found that there were those who loved coming earlier, there were those who loved coming later, and we were able to enlarge the total membership without enlarging the facilities or the staff. As an added benefit we now had two congregations supporting one facility. This meant that one of the congregations could support our local program and the surplus funds could be diverted into mission ventures. When we were later built to triple services, it was even more exciting, for we were able then to give two-thirds of our budget to missions while using only one-third of the total funds for our own local needs. This pattern continues to the present day.

And, then, I learned the fifth lesson for building a strong church. We were experiencing such growth and so many new converts that we soon caught the attention of our superiors. When a large church in our district had an opening, I was asked to take it. While in that church, a group became interested in the work of the Holy Spirit. They invited me to come and begin a Bible study in their homes, for they declared that they knew very little of the Bible apart from the readings in their prayer book. That Bible study soon grew so large that we had to break it into two.

The importance of having home Bible studies was an invaluable lesson. In these home Bible studies I developed a whole new style of teaching. Rather than the Sunday oratory style, I would just sit and talk in a very natural way. They would feel the freedom to interrupt when they did not understand a particular passage or interpretation of the passage, and it would turn into animated discussions. I found that their attention span was increased. In church after thirty minutes of preaching people were restless. But we could sit for an hour-and-a-half to two hours in the home and then the people would actually be disappointed that I stopped.

Later on when we started Calvary Chapel, we started several home Bible studies. The one on Monday night was geared for the young people and I would more or less "rap" with them as we sat in the living room of a home in Costa Mesa. The group soon became so large that we no longer fit in the home. Kids were sitting in the dining room, kitchen, up the stairway, in the entry hall, and there would be more outside who couldn't get in. We were, at that time, building our first chapel. The slab had been poured, so at night we would set up lights and the kids would sit on the slab and I would sit there with them. We just built the chapel walls up around them as time went on. It was during this time that we began to reach hundreds of the young people who had been involved in the hippie culture. They loved the informality of sitting outside and having the teacher just sit there and talk with them rather than preach at them.

From these informal talks I developed the style of teaching in a natural, almost conversational way. I just talk with the congregation about the things of God, of the glories of His nature, of His Kingdom. I found that if I'm talking—rather than preaching—the attention span holds for an hour as they sit with open Bibles learning God's Word. A half-hour of preaching can wear people out, but an hour of teaching, if it's done in an easy conversational way, does not.

These are not complicated lessons. In fact, the secret that I seek to impart to those eager to enter the ministry is to teach the Word of God simply. Tradition can be a hard thing to overcome, but lack of church growth can be more discouraging. It's been exciting to watch Calvary Chapels all across the country grow as the power of God touches people's lives. The harvest of souls into the Kingdom of God is our goal. May God ever receive the glory and honor due His name.

Another important principle that pastors learn at Calvary Chapel is complete dependence on the Holy Spirit to help them in expounding the Word. Jesus said that the Holy Spirit would teach them all things and bring to their remembrance the things that they had been taught. Paul said that the natural man could not understand the things of the Spirit neither could he know them for they were spiritually discerned. What is found at Calvary Chapel is the Spirit of God working through the Word of God to change the people of God.

There are many churches that offer excellent teaching of the Bible, but almost deny the current work of the Spirit of God. This creates dead orthodoxy. The people may be well versed in the

Scriptures but it has not altered their lifestyles to any great extent. They have a form of godliness but have denied the power.

On the other side of the coin are churches that emphasize the Holy Spirit but neglect teaching from the Word. This leads to emotionalism and an unstable condition that is open to every wind of doctrine and cunning craftiness of men who are standing by ready to deceive. Many heretical teachers have found fertile soil in church congregations that overemphasize only emotional experiences. It is so important to have a balance of the Word and the Spirit so that you can see the life-changing power of God at work and a stable growth of the Body of Christ.

At Calvary Chapel we have confidence that when God guides, God provides, so there is never an emphasis on money or giving. Many of our churches do not even pass the plate, but place a box at the entrance where the people who desire may contribute. God is never represented as being broke or facing imminent bankruptcy. The pastors have been taught that God is perfectly capable of supplying the needs for the things He desires to see accomplished. God does not need the support of His people to stay in business, the people need the support of God.

It is sad to see people driven away from the church by the appeals and gimmicks that have been used to solicit funds. Some have dropped out of church because they had nothing to give and felt embarrassed. We do not let this happen to them at Calvary because they are never asked to give or to pledge. As the apostle Paul said, never let your giving be by pressure or constraint, but let every man give as he has purposed in his own heart, for God loves a cheerful giver.

If you asked people who visited Calvary Chapel what impressed them the most, you would probably hear a variety of things, but some of the words that you would hear most often would be warm, loving, worshipful, casual. The first impression as you walk into the service is the warmth of God's love among His people. You see a lot of hugging, which probably goes back to the days of the hippies. There is a lot of happiness and laughter. There is also a reverent but casual atmosphere, which is reflected in the styles of clothes the people wear. They do not feel that they need to get dressed up to attend church. Yet if they are dressed up they do not feel uncomfortable. There is an acceptance of the person not the style of clothing. This again goes back to the hippie days when all kinds of clothes and styles were worn. Chuck Girard who was singing with the Love Song group in the earlier days of Calvary expressed it very well in his song "Little Country Church" with the lines:

> "Long hair, short hair
> Some coats and ties
> People finally coming around,
> Looking past the hair
> Straight into the eyes."

The music at Calvary Chapel is fresh and alive, and filled with worship choruses. Many times a worship group will lead the singing accompanied by guitars, drums, and keyboards. Many of the choruses are composed by the leaders in the worship groups and are passed on to the other Calvary Chapels. This gives quite a contemporary feel. Often a young person will share a song and explain that the Lord just gave him the song that afternoon.

Most of the churches in the U.S. today are highly organized and highly structured. By this I mean they stress the dependence that the church has on the people and the dependence the people have on the church. At Calvary Chapel we prefer a looser structure, as we stress our total dependency on God. It is interesting that most of the people in the U.S. today fit more comfortably into an independent, casual category, thus we fish almost alone in a huge, well-stocked pond, while many other churches try to fish in a much smaller pond.

In the book of Acts we are told that when the Church was born the believers continued steadfastly in the apostles' doctrine, fellowship, breaking of bread, and prayers. These are the four features that marked the early Church and these are the features that mark the Calvary Chapels. These are the things that are emphasized, sought after, and practiced, and we have discovered that—as in the early Church—the Lord adds to our numbers daily.

After seeing this work of the Lord with its remarkable fruit one is left with an obvious conclusion: "To God be the glory, great things He has done."

Ministry Information

1. CHUCK SMITH
Calvary Chapel Costa Mesa
3800 South Fairview
Santa Ana, CA 92704
(714) 979-4422
Website: www.calvarychapel.com/costamesa

2. GREG LAURIE
Harvest Christian Fellowship
6115 Arlington Avenue
Riverside, CA 92504
(951) 687-6902
Website: www.harvest.org

3. STEVE MAYS
Calvary Chapel South Bay
19300 South Vermont
Gardena, CA 90248
(310) 352-3333
Website: www.ccsouthbay.org

4. JON COURSON
Searchlight Ministry
P.O. Box 360
Jacksonville, OR 97530
(541) 899-9577
Website: www.joncourson.com

5. RAUL RIES
Calvary Chapel Golden Springs
22324 Golden Springs Drive
Diamond Bar, CA 91765
(909) 396-1884
Website: www.radio1@calvarygs.org

6. JEFF JOHNSON
Calvary Chapel Downey
12808 Woodruff Avenue
Downey, CA 90242
(562) 803-5631
Website: www.calvarychapel.org/downey

7. SKIP HEITZIG
Calvary of Albuequerque
4001 Osuna Road
NE Albuequerque, NM 87109
(505) 344-0880
Website: www.calvaryabq.org

8. BIL GALLATIN
Calvary Chapel of the Finger Lakes
1777 Rochester Road
Farmington, NY 14425
(585) 398-3550
Website: www.ccfingerlakes.org

9. JOE FOCHT
Calvary Chapel Philadelphia
13500 Philmont Avenue
Philadelphia, PA 19116
(215) 969-1520
Website: www.ccphilly.org

10. MIKE MACINTOSH
Horizon Christian Fellowship
5331 Mount Alifan Drive
P.O. Box 17480
San Diego, CA 92177-7480
(858) 277-4991
Website: www.horizonsd.org

Other Resources By Chuck Smith

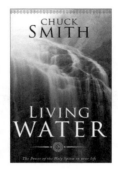

LIVING WATER

This book captures the message of God's ability to change lives through His Holy Spirit. The reader will grow deeply in the knowledge and understanding of the Holy Spirit; His grace, His love, His power, and His gifts. Also available in Spanish.

WHY GRACE CHANGES EVERYTHING

Through remarkable insight gleaned from the Bible and his own life, Pastor Chuck unfolds the mystery of grace. The reader will be refreshed and encouraged by the depth of God's grace toward us. Also available in Spanish.

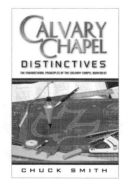

CALVARY CHAPEL DISTINCTIVES

Calvary Chapel values both the teaching of God's Word, as well as the work of the Holy Spirit. It is this balance that makes Calvary Chapel a distinct and uniquely blessed movement of God. Also available in Spanish.

TO ORDER CALL 1-800-272-WORD

LOVE THE MORE EXCELLENT WAY

In this rich, encouraging, and deeply practical book, Pastor Chuck describes how every one of us can come to experience and share the kind of world-changing love that continuously pours from the very heart of God, the original Lover Himself. Also available in Spanish.

OLD & NEW TESTAMENT GUIDES

Master the Old and New Testament quickly and easily using this verse-by-verse overview. Includes introductions, explanations, study questions, Greek word origin definitions, biblical maps, charts, and diagrams.

THE MAN GOD USES

Do you want to be used by God? In his warm personal style, Chuck Smith examines the personal characteristics of the people God used in the Book of Acts. *The Man God Uses* will lead you into a deeper spiritual walk, while helping you to understand God's plan for your life.

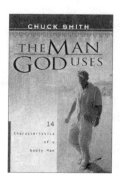

VISIT OUR WEB SITE: TWFT.COM

WISDOM FOR TODAY

Come alongside Pastor Chuck as he takes us on a journey from Genesis to Revelation. Providing God's wisdom for our lives in this daily devotional, discover how the Bible speaks volumes of wisdom to us every day.

PRAYER OUR GLORIOUS PRIVILEGE

It is easy to read a book on prayer and walk away unchanged. Recognize that prayer is the most potent weapon in your spiritual arsenal, and use it with great promise and much hope for when you begin a life of prayer, you begin a great adventure.

THE FINAL ACT

In *The Final Act,* Pastor Chuck Smith sets the stage for God s prophetic plan, providing insight into current world events leading up to one climactic battle that will usher in eternity. Explaining the rapture, the rise of the Antichrist, and conditions that favor the Lord's soon return, *The Final Act* is a compact, hard-hitting expose' on the last days of human history.

TO ORDER CALL 1-800-272-WORD

THE RAPTURE: ARE YOU READY?

One day millions of people, young and old, are going to be snatched away up into the air with Jesus Christ in heaven. Who is going? What will happen on earth after the rapture? Join Pastor Chuck as he expounds upon the Scriptures detailing the rapture of the church and the great tribulation.

HOW CAN A MAN BE BORN AGAIN?

It's a term we've all heard before. But do you really know what it means to be born again? And why did Jesus say that it was necessary to be born again if you want to see the kingdom of God? This book explains the difference between physical and spiritual birth. And why God created man in the first place—because in the end, it's not about religion—it's about a relationship. Available in Spanish.

For information about additional products
or to be added to our e-mail list
for product updates,
please contact:

THE WORD
FOR TODAY

P.O. Box 8000, Costa Mesa, CA 92628
800-272-WORD (9673)
www.twft.com • E-mail: info@twft.com